Around Every Corner of
CONNECTICUT

Around Every Corner of
CONNECTICUT
100 TOWNS TO EXPLORE EVERY SEASON

Sarah Cody

Globe
Pequot

Essex, Connecticut

Globe
Pequot

An imprint of The Globe Pequot Publishing Group, Inc.
64 South Main Street
Essex, CT 06426
www.globepequot.com

Distributed by NATIONAL BOOK NETWORK

British Library Cataloguing in Publication Information available

Library of Congress Cataloging-in-Publication Data
Names: Cody, Sarah, 1973– author.
Title: Around every corner of Connecticut : 100 towns to explore every
    season / Sarah Cody.
Other titles: Around every corner of Connecticut, one hundred towns to
    explore every season
Description: Essex, Connecticut : Globe Pequot, 2024. | Includes index. |
    Summary: "A celebration, with photos throughout, of the abundance of
    beautiful destinations and exciting seasonal (and year-round) activities
    in Connecticut"—Provided by publisher.
Identifiers: LCCN 2023043805 (print) | LCCN 2023043806 (ebook) | ISBN
    9781493076857 (paperback) | ISBN 9781493076864 (epub)
Subjects: LCSH: Connecticut—Guidebooks. | Cities and
    towns—Connecticut—Guidebooks. | Connecticut—History, Local.
Classification: LCC F92.3 C639 2024 (print) | LCC F92.3 (ebook) | DDC
    917.4604—dc23/eng/20231023
LC record available at https://lccn.loc.gov/2023043805
LC ebook record available at https://lccn.loc.gov/2023043806

Dedication

Around Every Corner of Connecticut is dedicated to my father, who always wanted me to write a book. Well-read and smart, he was full of interesting nuggets of information during our long conversations. He enjoyed hearing about my travels while reporting and always had suggestions of new places for me to visit. I wish I could tell you all about Weir Farm, Dad. You were right; it really is spectacular.

CONTENTS

Sunset views from a boat off the coast of Westbrook.

Introduction

Sails, billowing from sleek boats in Long Island Sound. Vibrant colors on display from a unique overlook on a crisp day. A deer, peeking around a gnarled tree on a snowy path in the woods. Daffodils blooming around a historic home as birds chirp during those first days of warmth. This is Connecticut, a beautiful state to enjoy every season, all year long.

I started my news reporting job in the Nutmeg State in the late 1990s, focused on covering fires, accidents, crimes, you name it. But pretty soon, thanks to a series called *Daytrippers*, I began traveling the state, highlighting all it has to offer: the unique landmarks, the cool museums, the adventurous activities, and, of course, the gorgeous vistas from shoreline to farmland. I grew to love every nook and cranny of the state. And I grew a reputation too. As my expertise increased, friends and viewers would routinely reach out. "Hey, Sarah, relatives are coming to visit. Where should I take them?" I love this role and eventually realized I could share my knowledge with a wider audience through the written page. Hence, *Around Every Corner of Connecticut* was born!

So, if you're home with the family, looking for something unique to do, allow me to help. This book, split into fun, seasonal sections, provides a comprehensive look at my favorite locations from the Litchfield Hills to New London's shores. Take a friendly llama for a hike, or spy a majestic bald eagle sitting in a tree on the banks of the Connecticut River. Maybe a sleigh ride through a snowy pasture is more your speed. Speaking of speed, did you know you can take an adventurous UTV ride, right here in our state? And guess what? Connecticut even boasts a Dinosaur Trail! If your kids are anything like my boys, they'll love it.

Over my twenty-five years in the media business here in Connecticut, I've been lucky enough to rack up a virtual Rolodex of amazing contacts who can speak wisely about our beautiful landscape and interesting museums. As John Proto, executive director of the Shore Line Trolley Museum, says, these destinations aren't just about fun (although that's certainly important). They're integral to our education. They boost our local economy.

I grew up in Carlisle, Massachusetts, next to Concord, and had a strong attachment to the history of the area. Strolling over the North Bridge and past Nathaniel Hawthorne's house was a common route for me. In fact, I worked summers giving tours at the Orchard House, where author Louisa May Alcott wrote the classic *Little Women*. It was a family affair. My mother worked at the museum for forty years. So colonial homes and old stories are in my blood. While I love zipping through the trees or riding a Segway around the shoreline, I really got a kick out of

Sailboat races in Essex harbor.

learning more about the state's history as this book unfolded. And during these tumultuous, changing times, I was intrigued to learn more about Connecticut's early social justice warriors like Harriet Beecher Stowe, writing in the 1800s about racial inequality. There were other women, way ahead of their time, making strides in a man's world. Read ahead to learn about the significant contributions of Frances Osborne Kellogg, Theodate Pope Riddle, and Martha A. Parsons—all leaders in their fields.

While writing this book, I revisited spots that I knew well, places like the Mystic Seaport Museum and the Dinosaur Place, where I had cherished memories with my family. But I also found new destinations, such as the Old Drake Bridge and the Glebe House, which piqued my interest and led me to learning more about this state, now my home, better than ever before. And it was an interesting time to write *Around Every Corner of Connecticut*, when some destinations had reinvented themselves during the pandemic, creating ways to stay open while keeping visitors safe. Many of those tactics proved successful and stuck, breathing new life and creativity into existing experiences.

I have always been passionate about covering issues surrounding those with special needs. So this book provides activities and locations for people of all abilities, highlighting places where everyone can thrive, learn, and relax. You will read the term "ADA compliant" when I write about the many locations that have adhered to the Americans with Disabilities Act, providing accommodations and access to those who may require special accommodations. In writing this book, I discovered that this has been nearly impossible for some of our historic destinations, but many are working to improve conditions where they can and are willing to work with families to find solutions.

Don't expect this to be your average guidebook! *Around Every Corner of Connecticut* features interviews with museum directors, history buffs, authors, and farmers—all the wonderful people who make our lively tourism scene tick. Their insight gives our locations a perspective and personality that are truly unique. Plus, you'll find some personal recommendations from this mom of two spirited boys who were always on the go: skiing at our local resorts, ziplining through the trees, and reaching into every available touch tank. I've even included some personal photos from our treasured outings over the years.

Let's find an adventure around every corner! There are so many incredible places to explore.

Fields of Essex in the winter snow

Winter

When the days get shorter and the temperatures drop, don't just grab a blanket, turn on the TV, and hibernate. Connecticut boasts some great spots for outdoor activities from cross-country skiing to ice fishing. So don the winter coat, gloves, hat, and maybe binoculars, and find a cold-weather adventure to beat the winter blues!

Essex: The holiday season brings a special glow to this beautiful town; the main street is lined with white lights, illuminating the historic homes and quaint shops. It's a time that brings tons of tourists to a spot just outside the village, the **Essex Steam Train & Riverboat (www.essex steamtrain.com)**, which hosts the North Pole Express. Over the years, this has grown into an incredibly popular holiday tradition for thousands of visitors each season. Making a reservation is like buying a ticket to the newest, hottest concert! You have to act fast! All reservations are now made online. Board at the station, swathed in decorations, for an interactive trip to the North Pole, featuring elves that sing and tell stories, along with a visit from Mr. and Mrs. Claus. "We present a good family-oriented event. Everyone can come: Grandma, Grandpa, aunts, uncles, cousins," says Bob Wuchert, vice president of Essex Steam Train & Riverboat. "It's beautiful, just seeing the faces of the children, even the parents. Maybe they were here thirty or forty years ago for their first Santa train experience and they're back with their children." It is truly a magical experience, one that we enjoyed with our two sons for many years. The station is ADA compliant, but the restored historic trains were not built with accessibility in mind. It is possible for those with mobility issues to contact Customer Service to discuss options for riding the train. Down the way at the **Connecticut River Museum (www.ctriver museum.org)**, the fun surrounding locomotives continues. An annual train show, created by local artist Steve Cryan, delights visitors young and old. Cryan, a musician, painter, and tour guide, builds an intricate display that's really incredible. "It's full of detail and hilarity. It's a wonderful place for people of all generations to come and really look, look again, and look even more closely to find every tiny detail," says Elizabeth

Left: Every winter, see an intricate toy train display at the Connecticut River Museum. Right: My sons, Sam and Ben, enjoy a ride on the North Pole Express with Mrs. Claus.

Left: Connecticut offers some great spots for cutting down your own Christmas tree. Right: Each year, thousands of visitors to the Essex Steam Train ride the North Pole Express. Tom Nanos Photography

Kaeser, executive director of the museum. Several HO scale model trains chug past seascapes and through the countryside on the main layout. Cryan funnels his sense of humor into an I-Spy game where participants must look hard to find dinosaurs or Santas nestled into the mini landscape. The museum sports an elevator, making it possible for those in a wheelchair to see the display. Folks can also take a Winter Wildlife Eagle Cruise during February and March on **Riverquest**, acquired by the museum in 2022. "*Riverquest* stays on the water year-round when most people pack their boats up," says Kaeser. "When the *Riverquest* goes out, there really aren't any other watercraft out there, and it feels like nothing else." These cruises are a great way to enjoy winter on the water and spy majestic bald eagles, our nation's symbol of freedom, flying through the sky or sitting in a tree. "You get to see how they look and how they swoop and soar; it's incredible," says Kaeser. Essex now sports some resident bald eagles, but birds from all around make their way to this area due to its brackish water that never fully freezes, making it easy for the birds to fish and eat. An on-board naturalist shares interesting facts and stories. Bundle up! Coffee and binoculars are included in the ticket price. The boat cruises are accessible for most mobility levels. (Learn more about *Riverquest* in the "Fall" section of this book.)

Haddam: Another place to spot these majestic birds is, appropriately, **Eagle Landing State Park (portal.ct.gov/DEEP/State-Parks/Parks/ Eagle-Landing-State-Park)**, a gorgeous spot with sixteen acres along the Connecticut River sporting incredible views of the **Goodspeed Opera House (www.goodspeed.org)** and the famous swing bridge. "You can see beyond the bridge, up to the mouth of the Salmon River," says Jerry Connolly, who owns the **Audubon Shop (www.theaudubonshop.com)** in Madison along with his wife, Janet. Each year they bring a group to this area, one of Connecticut's newest state parks, to view bald eagles. "For the last dozen years, there's been an eagle's nest at the end of the airstrip across the way in East Haddam," he says, explaining the unique landscape that includes a small airport. "They return to the same nest each year, the male and the female, and they remain mated for life." Tour boats also come and go from this vantage point. The park includes walkways and docks that help folks relax and enjoy this unique area, but it is not accessible for those with mobility issues. Other natural spots in town, **Haddam Island State Park (portal.ct.gov/DEEP/State -Parks/Locate-Park-Forest/Other -State-Parks-and-Forests#HaddamIsl)**, **Haddam Meadows State Park (portal .ct.gov/DEEP/State-Parks/Parks/ Haddam-Meadows-State-Park)**, and **George Dudley Seymour State Park (portal.ct.gov/DEEP/State-Parks /Parks/George-Dudley-Seymour-State -Park)** allow visitors the chance to bird-watch, fish, and go boating. Also, be sure to check out **Cockaponset State Forest (portal.ct.gov/DEEP/ State-Parks/Forests/Cockaponset-State-Forest)**, Connecticut's second-largest state forest, great for cross-country skiing and snowmobiling in wintertime.

A beautiful bald eagle rests atop a tree along the Connecticut River.

During the holiday season, downtown Chester is alive with glowing stars.

Chester: What started as a pandemic project, bringing light to the lovely village of Chester, has grown and expanded to now be part of the town's fabric. **Starry Nights (www.visitchesterct.com/comeseestarrynights)** started as a bunch of sponsored stars, bought then displayed in honor of a loved one. But now, more than 150 stars adorn shops, restaurants, stone walls, and more to make this already beautiful downtown stretch seem downright magical in the winter. Additionally, peruse the **Chester Holiday Market (www.visitchesterct.com/events/chester-holiday -market-af5r3)** each Sunday between Thanksgiving and Christmas in the village. Find foods like baked goods and cheeses, along with craft items. Occasionally, Mrs. Claus will even stroll through the crowd. Finally, on a Sunday prior to Christmas, locals flock to the downtown area to see Santa cruise into town on a fire truck to visit eager children. Another unique spot in Chester is **Chakana Sky Alpacas (www.chakanaskyalpacas .com)**, an unassuming farm with a big mission. Owner Bill Bernhart named his farm to honor the indigenous people of the Andes Mountains, the native home of alpacas. Seventeen furry residents roam the fields, greeting people in a display of what Bernhart calls Farm Tourism. "When COVID hit, I decided to pivot and switch to private visits by appointment to give people a safe and fun place to go. It worked out really well," he says, noting that he saw about eighteen hundred people in three years. "Alpacas are native to South America. Though they've been domesticated for a good thousand years or more, they're still basically at heart a wild animal. They're very cautious with humans until you've built up a level of trust." Bernhart believes they really like the small visitors. "They're very curious about young kids because they're basically at eye level with the alpacas. They appreciate that. They don't find that threatening. They usually give kids an alpaca kiss," he says. An on-site "Paca-tique" sells products made of alpaca fiber. The farm is accessible by wheelchair or walker. Bernhart has future plans to start Alpaca Walks, where folks lead the animal on a stroll around the property.

Deep River: The third town in this tri-town area also offers some interesting winter fun. **Bushy Hill Nature Center** (**www.bushyhill.org**), located at the Incarnation Center, sports 740 acres with incredible hiking trails past streams and native plants, open to the public September through June. See woodlands, wetlands, and a fascinating wigwam site. I've always particularly loved the Maple Sugar Shack House, emitting incredible scents during February and March, teaching the public the fine art of making syrup. "Especially right now, with the sustainability movement and getting back to your roots, it connects you to that old world," says former director Jen Malaguti, now head teacher at the Steward School, on Bushy Hill's property. "This is a gift the Native Americans gave us. It's cross cultures now. It's a nice way to see how nature and humans can interact." During open-house weekends and school tours, naturalists at Bushy Hill teach the process of making sap into our favorite topping for pancakes and waffles. They tap trees and

Left: See how trees are tapped and maple syrup is made at Bushy Hill Nature Center in Deep River. Top right and bottom right: This large thrift store with a library, café, and animal sanctuary is fast becoming a popular destination.

then show how the sap is boiled down, over many hours, to become syrup. It's a great activity for all family members—including those of all abilities—and folks can head home with pints and half-pints of delicious New England syrup. This quaint town along the Connecticut River is also home to a unique spot that shares history, provides great shopping, and gives sanctuary to animals. The **Pandemonium Rainforest Project** (**www.pandemoniumrainforestproject.org**) is housed in an original Pratt Reed Ivory Mill. In the 1900s Deep River was home to the largest ivory trade in the United States. When founder Allison Sloane bought this building in 2021, her mission was to preserve the complicated history of the twelve-thousand-square-foot space while also, now, using it for good. "We want to teach people that this is a very precious, very small Earth, and we need to look toward our history for our future," says Sloane. Today this spot, which once exploited elephants, is used as an animal sanctuary. Money raised in the massive thrift shop supports rescued parrots and reptiles, on display for visitors to see. This location also boasts a cozy library, a café, a koi pond, a museum, and an outdoor space for musicians. It's fast becoming a destination. "We have people coming from all over New England now," says Sloane. "It's so exciting." The upstairs of the mill and the animal sanctuary are wheelchair accessible.

Burlington: Another place to experience maple sugaring toward the end of winter is **Lamothe's Sugar House (www.lamothesugarhouse.com)**. Rob Lamothe started producing syrup on his small working farm in 1971, with seven taps and an open fire. One day, a man asked if he could buy a quart of syrup. "I sold it to him. He was delighted; so was I. I knew we could make a business of it," he says. Now he runs the largest commercial syrup-making operation in the state. "We've got twenty-six miles of tubing in the woods and fifty-six hundred taps out," he says. He also has a state-of-the-art facility where the scientific process of filtering and purifying takes place.

Rob Lamothe runs the largest commercial maple syrup–making operation in Connecticut.

When the sap is running, this destination holds demonstrations for the public. "Our tour is free; the kids get lollipops, and the parents get hot coffee or mulled cider. What they get out of it is genuine New England charm," says Lamothe. Peruse the gift shop with syrup and tons of maple candy! The shop and production floor are wheelchair accessible. Nearby, find **Sessions Woods Wildlife Management Area (portal.ct.gov/DEEP/ Wildlife/Wildlife-Mangement-Areas/Sessions-Woods-Wildlife -Management-Area)**, where you can hike trails, check out a beaver dam, and explore an observation tower. Visitors are advised to be "Bear Aware" and to learn safety practices, in case they encounter this animal, before embarking on the trails. There are also indoor exhibits, intended to educate visitors and encourage them to peacefully coexist with area wildlife that has lost much of its natural habitat to development. Sessions Woods routinely hosts school groups and puts on demonstrations for the public. Folks can visit this location, which is ADA compliant, entirely for free. And don't miss a stop at a beloved location, **Hogan's Cider Mill (www.hoganscidermill.com)**, which opens for the season in February. Folks in wheelchairs are able to access the outdoor grounds and the first floor of the barns. But this spot is best known for its fascinating cider-making demonstrations in the fall. (See "Unique Outings for Fall" for more information.)

Ridgefield: The colder months are a great time to catch up on that movie intake. My favorite theater in the state just happens to be in the historic town of Ridgefield. The **Prospector (www.prospectortheater .org)** started as a movie theater providing meaningful employment to those of all abilities. "This was started because there's still a staggering figure in the country that roughly 80 percent of Americans with disabilities don't have jobs. We don't think that's OK," says Director of Operations and Technology Ryan Wenke, noting that the employees, called "Prospects," are paired with whatever job will allow them to "sparkle." "We teach and train through a wide array of jobs. We have box office concessions, a café, and a kitchen. We have a production team that films in-house videos that show before the movies. We have a landscaping

The Prospector, employing those of all abilities, is a state-of-the-art first-run movie theater.

team." Thus far, more than three hundred people of all abilities have been employed here. This cool mission is matched by its cool location, built prior to opening in 2014. "It was very important to us to have a building that matched the beauty of our mission and the people that work here," says Wenke, describing the light, bright lobby, filled with sculptures and mosaics. Folks often dress up like Spider-Man or Darth Vader at this first-run theater. And you might just hear the tunes of a local band playing in the lobby. It's just got a fantastic vibe. The theater serves some great food too. During the shutdown of the pandemic, the

Discover new artists at the Aldrich Contemporary Art Museum. Jason Mandella

Prospector, a nonprofit, spread its wings, producing delicious gourmet popcorn, now being shipped all around the country. The twenty-six-thousand-square-foot facility with state-of-the-art projectors is fully accessible for those with physical disabilities. It's in the heart of Ridgefield's gorgeous downtown, with tons of vibrant restaurants and shops. Find more culture at the **Ridgefield Playhouse** (**www.ridgefieldplayhouse.org**), featuring shows by such famous artists as Keb Mo', Rita Rudner, and the Glenn Miller Orchestra, along with children's programs and first-run movies. The playhouse is accessible to all. Also peruse the sights at the **Aldrich Contemporary Art Museum** (**www.thealdrich.org**), known to show cutting-edge pieces. "The Aldrich is a really special place. We're one of the oldest contemporary art museums in the country. We are an incubator for contemporary art. So we're really the place you're going to go to discover new artists," says Director of Marketing and Communications Emily Devoe. "We're the only museum dedicated solely to presenting contemporary art in the state of Connecticut." The museum is open year-round every day of the week except Tuesday. On the third Saturday of every month, admission is free to the public, with special tours and family programs. Folks can also create their own art in an on-site studio. This location is fully accessible.

Litchfield: Looking for a quintessential New England town, perfect for a brisk walk that leads to buying holiday presents then a cozy dinner in front of a fire? Look no further than beautiful Litchfield (**www**

The streets of downtown Litchfield are particularly charming in the wintertime.

.visitlitchfieldct.com), known as a Connecticut gem, with a picturesque main street and town green. "We have a festive holiday stroll every year. Folks mill about in town. We have carol singing with the high school students. We have a tree lighting, and the local historical society has an ornament-making workshop for the kids," says Lindsey Turner, vice chair of the Litchfield Economic Development Commission, which runs **VisitLitchfieldCT.com**, developed during the pandemic. "Litchfield is such an extraordinary place, and people don't even know it is here. We want to curate experiences for people so that they know what to do. You come into a new town, you might drive through and have no idea what there is for you to do. We want people to feel like their hands are held a little bit with that experience." Find at least six antiques shops, as well as establishments for clothes, flowers, and home decor. But Litchfield's charm extends well beyond the downtown area. The **White Memorial Conservation Center (www.whitememorialcc.org)** offers four thousand acres of outdoor fun in nature. From birding to biking, there are activities for every season. There's an incredible boardwalk trail around a pond. And in winter it's a very special place to break out the cross-country skis and traverse more than forty miles of trails through both wooded areas and gorgeous fields. "Litchfield's natural resources are one of our biggest assets. I think it's something that draws people to live here and also visit here," says Turner, who also mentions **Topsmead State Forest** (**portal.ct.gov/DEEP/State-Parks/Forests/Topsmead-State -Forest**) as a unique destination. Named for its location atop a meadow, the property includes a beautiful English Tudor–style house, built in 1925. In the offseason, enjoy hiking, birding, and cross-country skiing on the grounds. "It's just spectacular," says Turner. Head to **Bees, Fleas & Trees** (**www.beesfleasandtrees.com**) to pick out the perfect Christmas tree. Kids can write letters to Santa Claus as they drink some creamy hot chocolate. "While it is a historic town, it's a living, breathing, vibrant place," says Turner. "I want everybody to experience just a snippet of the joy it is to live here."

Morris: Next door to Litchfield, Morris is known for a sport that requires patience, warm clothes, and quick hands: ice fishing. Icy Bantam Lake is a popular spot for setting up camp, and when I say "camp," some people go all out. Think tents, stoves, firepits, and spreads of gourmet food. Experts say bass, pike, perch, and trout usually bite the most during the morning hours. Enthusiasts drill a hole in the ice with a manual auger. Folks place a tip-up over each hole. This is an apparatus including a reel, a line, and an orange "alert" flag that pops up when a fish is hooked. Then participants rely on a ruler! Per state requirement, "keepers" must be at least twenty-eight inches long. "Here at Bantam Lake, the largest natural lake in Connecticut, you just drive up, park in a dirt parking area, and the lake is all around you. It's amazing, and I don't think people realize the level of access there is to Bantam Lake," says Doug Clement, a writer who lives in Morris. "When you get out on the lake, it's an entirely different experience and an entirely different perspective. Everything that seems familiar to you in the landscape is suddenly completely different. It's really surprising and fun." The Morris side of Bantam Lake sports great views of Apple Hill, part of the four-thousand-acre **White Memorial Conservation Center** preserve. Ice fishing is a great way to bond with friends and appreciate nature in the wintertime. "It's fishing for sport. I get the sense watching them that it's not even so much about fishing, it's more of a lifestyle ritual," says Clement. Refer to Connecticut's **Department of Environmental Protection** website (**https://portal .ct.gov/DEEP/Fishing/General-Information/Ice-Fishing**) for more instructions and locations. Participants need to purchase a license. Other locations of note in Morris are **Camp Columbia State Park** (**https:// portal.ct.gov/DEEP/State-Parks/Parks/Camp-Columbia-State-Park**

Each winter, Bantam Lake is filled with tents, grills, and gear during ice fishing season. Douglas Clement

-**Forest**), a beautiful spot for hiking. Visitors can even bring dogs. Also check out **Mount Tom State Park (portal.ct.gov/DEEP/State-Parks/Parks/Mount-Tom-State-Park**), in Morris, Litchfield, and Washington, where folks can also ice-skate. Clement recommends hiking a trail up to a stone tower. "People don't really know about Mount Tom State Park; it's kind of a secret place," he says. "People don't think of it for winter activity, and it's really kind of great out there and quiet." He tells folks to look around. Morris is filled with natural opportunities. "There are all of these undiscovered gems," says Clement. "These hikes are great in the winter because nobody else is out there. The wildlife is fantastic. You see deer, coyotes, and bobcats."

Bethlehem: A visit to Connecticut's very own Little Town of Bethlehem is a special wintertime activity. "We're called the Christmas Town; that's our nickname," says Meghan Bove, director of the town's historical society. People come from all around to have their Christmas cards sent from the town's post office. "At its peak, it brought sixty-thousand people to town. It was huge. It's not that big anymore, but it's still a draw from area towns," adds Vincent Bove, also part of the historical society. Folks are looking for two things: the postmark plus a special cancellation stamp, a festive touch during this special time. The Town Green features a lovely, life-size Nativity scene for families to gaze upon, reflecting on the classic

Bethlehem is called the Christmas Town for several reasons, including the Nativity scene on the green.

Christmas story. Each year on the first weekend of December, the town holds the Christmas Town Festival, which came about in the 1980s when townsfolk were looking for a way to fund the rebuilding of Memorial Hall, the town hall, after a devastating fire. Plenty of money was raised, saving taxpayer dollars, and the tradition continued. The festival features craft booths, visits with Santa, hayrides, and the lighting of the town Christmas tree. "Our tree is actually bigger than the one in Rockefeller Center," Vincent says proudly of the tree that's usually around ninety feet tall. "When it gets lit in our small, little town that has that colonial charm, it's kind of special." Vincent believes this town, nestled in the Litchfield Hills, where he's lived his whole life, is filled with a unique, rich history. "It reaches one thousand feet above sea level, so we're high enough that we get snow when the other towns don't. Everything about the town has a special draw to it." Visitors can also travel to the **Abbey of Regina Laudis (www.abbeyofreginalaudis.org)**, built after World War II, to see a crèche made in Italy in the 1700s. "It's gorgeous, and a lot of people don't even know about it," says Meghan. It's housed in a barn donated to the abbey by Caroline Ferriday, who also donated her incredible, storied home to the Antiquarian Society. Originally built in the 1750s for Pastor Joseph Bellamy, the man who helped establish the town, the house has gained modern-day notoriety thanks to a best-selling historical novel called *Lilac Girls* by Martha Hall Kelly. The **Bellamy-Ferriday House & Garden (www.ctlandmarks.org/properties/bellamy-ferriday-house -garden/)** is open for tours during spring, summer, and fall. Ferriday was a twentieth-century philanthropist. During World War II, she organized medical aid for survivors of the Ravensbrück concentration camp. The house is fascinating, as are the gardens, featuring rare plants. "It's a gem, right in the middle of town," says Meghan, noting that the eighty-acre-plus property includes walking paths through a preserve that is open year-round.

New Hartford: In the winter, my family always loved to jump in the car for a spontaneous trip to spend a day at **Ski Sundown** (**www.ski sundown.com**). Local ski areas really serve such an important purpose. They're great places for kids and adults alike to learn the challenging sport of skiing or snowboarding. "We really do pride ourselves on being a family mountain. It's one of those sports you can do with a family; you can do it lifelong. It's just passed down generation to generation," says owner Bob Switzgable. "We have anywhere from 100 to 180 instructors every year." Once kids know how to ski, the smaller, nearby areas are

Ski Sundown in New Hartford has a robust learn-to-ski program for those of all abilities. Ski Sundown

fantastic spots for wholesome outdoor fun, even on weekday afternoons, after school. And Sundown has it all: trails for all levels, a nice cafeteria, and an incredible adaptive program for people with disabilities. "It's just taking off, it's terrific," says Switzgable. There's also a well-known ski group for women—where females, maybe moms, can fine-tune their skills whether they're new or rusty. Each year, this group becomes like a sisterhood, getting together off the slopes for outings and potluck dinners. Ski Sundown, which has been in operation for more than fifty years, boasts seventy ski-able acres with three triple chairlifts, two conveyors, and night skiing. Even when Mother Nature doesn't provide adequate conditions, Sundown's snowmaking machines are working full blast, while staff makes sure the trails are covered. New Hartford is also home to two vineyards, **Jerram Winery** (**www.jerramwinery.com**) and

Connecticut Valley Winery (**www.ctvalleywinery.com**), both accessible for all and open for tastings. For real adventurers, check out **Berkshire Balloons** (**www.berkshireballoons.com**), taking folks high in the sky for a view of Connecticut that won't soon be forgotten! Private flights, with a maximum of four people, are offered year-round and typically take off during the early-morning hours from New Hartford or Bethlehem. They last about one hour. "It's very common for people to call me up and say, 'I've wanted to do this my whole life but never knew it was available to the general public,'" says owner and pilot Robert Zirpolo. Also, find cross-country skiing, letterboxing, hiking, and more at beautiful **Nepaug State Forest** (**portal.ct.gov/-/media/DEEP/stateparks/maps/backpacking/NepaugCampSite2pdf.pdf**).

Derby: Another "quintessentially New England" activity is, of course, ice-skating. Mother Nature needs to cooperate with some of those frigid temps, but once she does, there's nothing better than donning those cozy

The beautiful Osborne Homestead Museum hosts special holiday tours.

duds and skates for a glide around one of Connecticut's beautiful ponds. **Osbornedale State Park** (**portal.ct.gov/DEEP/State-Parks/Parks/Osbornedale-State-Park**) is a well-known spot for this sport. In the wintertime, folks also love to cross-country ski and hike around this beautiful area, through fields that were once a dairy farm belonging to Frances Osborne Kellogg, a female trailblazer in conservation, business, and agriculture in the mid-1800s. Her Colonial Revival home, now the **Osborne Homestead Museum** (**portal.ct.gov/DEEP/Education/Kellogg/Osborne-Homestead-Museum**), is listed on the National Register of Historic Places. While its regular season runs from May through October, the museum is open the Friday after Thanksgiving through the Saturday before Christmas for holiday tours. "Volunteers decorate the museum with different themes," says museum curator Susan Robinson. "The themes revolve around history, art, and the environment." She believes the museum's mission really resonates with the public, especially nowadays. "We focus on women's history. The majority of historic house museums do not focus on women's history, so we tell the story of a woman who was ahead of her time; who, before women got the right to vote, was running her family's businesses. She was running a dairy farm and was really paving her own way." In fact, she donated funds to create the Frances E. Osborne Kellogg Dairy Center on the campus of the University of Connecticut in Storrs, a bustling agricultural destination. Due to the historic nature of the building, the museum is not wheelchair accessible.

Enjoy winter by going skating at Osbornedale State Park.

Southington: Mount Southington (**www.mountsouthington.com**) provides fantastic opportunities for families as well. This local ski area has a cool vibe. "We have fourteen trails with a variety of terrain from wide-open slopes to real narrow classic New England skiing. We have a top-to-bottom terrain park," says President and General Manager Jay Dougherty. "It offers an opportunity to get out and be healthy. It's great to be able to spend that time together with your family outdoors." The ski area, known for its learn-to-ski programs, special events, and night skiing, has been a local staple for family fun for nearly sixty years. "Grandparents started skiing here, then their children; now the grandkids are here," says Dougherty. Mount Southington works with an organization called Leaps of Faith to provide instruction to veterans and kids with special needs. Another spot in Southington is sure to engage the whole family: **Bradley Mountain Farm** (**www.bradleymountainfarm.com**). The farm burst onto the tourism scene a few years ago, just in time to provide an outlet for families during the pandemic. "Bradley Mountain Farm is all about connecting people with opportunities to meet livestock in different ways," says owner Anneliese Dadras of the two-hundred-year-old farm, started by one of Southington's founding fathers. "What we try to do the most is create experiences for people and generate nostalgia, teach people about the past." Activities with goats allow folks to get up-close and personal with animals. In winter, Dadras fires up a pellet stove in a barn and hosts activities like goat snuggles, goat yoga, cuddle therapy, and "make-n-take" soap workshops. She also hosts holiday activities, such as "reindeer" goat photos, in the Bradley House. During the warmer months, folks can take a goat for a stroll around the beautiful farmland, through fields, and even past scenic Crescent Lake, where a pair of bald eagles live

Left: Mount Southington provides a great atmosphere for family skiing in Connecticut. Mount Southington
Right: Take a holiday picture with a "reindeer" goat at Bradley Mountain Farm. Bradley Mountain Farm

in the trees. The farm often hosts full-moon walks. A visit here means more than just seeing a goat. "They're not just an animal to pet and then leave. They're animals that add to your life. We have people with autism who come here; senior citizens who come from nursing homes, and they remember when they grew up on farms," says Dadras, noting the magic that animals bring to a child with disabilities. "Animals don't need words to communicate. Animals don't need words to show love. Most of their communication is nonverbal. They just give the love back in big quantities. We have parents who say their kids just blossomed while they're here."

Middlefield: Powder Ridge Mountain Park & Resort (www.powder ridgepark.com) holds a special place in my heart, mainly because of its backstory. The property had been closed and abandoned for many years when the Hayes family, behind the popular summer destination Brownstone Adventure Sports Park, bought the property and revitalized it with tons of energy and high hopes. And they did not disappoint. With a mission to offer big-mountain amenities close to home, the lodge features the usual cafeteria but also a bar area with spirits for parents watching from the sidelines. Upstairs, take it up a notch at Fire at the Ridge, an upscale restaurant with seafood appetizers and fine cuts of meat for the main course. This location even hosts weddings, special events, and outdoor dining igloos

Find skiing, tubing, and great restaurants with outdoor dining at Powder Ridge Mountain Park & Resort. Powder Ridge

28

in the cold weather. In terms of skiing, there are plenty of trails for all levels. Powder Ridge also provides lessons to those with special needs. Folks can even rent a unique snow bike that is attached to skis. This apparatus works well for some people with knee or ankle problems. Use of the bike requires a sixty-minute lesson, which leads to a certification card. Tubing has emerged as another really popular activity at Powder Ridge. With a variety of lanes, bright lights, and loud music, letting go and flying down an icy path is incredibly freeing! It's exhilarating for kids and adults alike. In the warm weather, Powder Ridge is well-known for its mountain biking trails. And while

Lyman Orchards (www.lyman orchards.com) is also known for summer activities such as berry picking, it remains very vibrant in winter, hosting Goat Strolls, featuring animals from Southington's Bradley Mountain Farm. Visitors can also partake in Connecticut-made food tastings in the Apple Barrel Farm Market and occasional Homestead Tours, where folks can see inside the founding family's historic home from 1864. "We try to bring people out twelve months a year to Middlefield," says Executive Vice President John Lyman. "We're trying to be creative and offer events that appeal to all

A great destination year-round, Lyman Orchards offers some fun and unique winter events. Lyman Orchards

people." Lyman also hosts children's events, such as a Kids' Valentine's Heart Cake Decorating workshop, Animal Tracking workshops, and maple sugaring demos for the public. When in Middlefield, be sure to visit **Wadsworth Falls State Park (portal.ct.gov/DEEP/State-Parks/Parks/ Wadsworth-Falls-State-Park)**, great for hiking and biking on those mild winter days. Revelers can also see a scenic waterfall.

Cornwall: This beautiful town is home to **Mohawk Mountain (www .mohawkmtn.com)**, the oldest and biggest ski area in the state of Connecticut. Called "the home of snowmaking," it is usually the first resort in the state to have its trails covered each season. There are more than thirty trails, with about eight that run top to bottom, for all levels.

Mohawk Mountain is the oldest and biggest ski resort in Connecticut. Daniel Hedden

"A lot of local families have had kids grow up, work here, learn to ski here, go off to other mountains, and always end up coming back, so it's a unique spot," says manager Dan Hedden. "We offer rental packages for people who want to try skiing, also beginner lessons as well as more advanced lessons. We offer race teams and children's programs. For our children's programs, we have people come from all over; they'll drive hours to get here every weekend so their kids can learn to ski and develop their skills." Lessons are inclusive to those with special needs. The mountain also hosts events and training for the Special Olympics. Mohawk features something for everyone, with a great tubing course and night skiing. Despite this big attraction, Cornwall is a small town, known for its charm, not so much for its vast array of activities. "It's a nice morning or afternoon stroll through the little town," says Connecticut tourism expert Janet Serra, who recommends a stop at **Cornwall Bridge Pottery** (**www.cbpots.com**), featuring work by artist Todd Piker. "He learned to make pots in England," says Serra. Up the street from the store, find Piker's actual studio. "A couple times a year, he fires up his huge kiln and invites the public to watch him work," says Serra, a fan of these special events. In West Cornwall, find one of the state's nine covered bridges, always delightful to see. "West Cornwall Bridge is one of two that can actually be crossed by auto traffic," says Serra, noting that the other one is Bull's Bridge in Kent. On mild days, rent a bike at **Covered Bridge Electric Bike** (**www .coveredbridgeebike.com**) to see this lovely area in style while getting exercise, despite the electric boost! This shop, with additional locations in North Canaan and Kent, even offers guided e-bike tours.

Salisbury: In this country town you'll find a winter event that's entirely unique, one you won't find anywhere else in the state. **Jumpfest** (**www .jumpfest.org**) is an annual ski jump competition that takes place every February; visitors can watch some of the best Olympic hopefuls compete on Satre Hill. Imagine this: a tower standing seventy feet atop the hill. If that's not terrifying enough, the jumpers perch on a bar that's 350 feet above the snowy land. They then literally whip down a three hundred-foot run, picking up speed before they soar through the air at around fifty miles per hour, delighting spectators. "They have cow bells that ring, so they're ringing these bells as the skiers are going down this hill, and literally they fly, right before your eyes," says Janet Serra, who has worked on the Connecticut tourism scene for more than thirty-five years. She notes that the vibe at Jumpfest is family-friendly: "They have big bonfires going and people drink hot chocolate; it's just convivial." Salisbury is one of only six locations on the East Coast to offer such an event. Prior to the competition on Friday night, spectators can watch a wild and wacky Human Dog Sled Race. Teams of six people compete for prizes. Also, in the Taconic section of Salisbury, find **Bear Mountain**, the highest mountain that fully lies within Connecticut. A 6.1-mile hiking trail takes about three and a half hours to complete. "Even my dog was exhausted! My German shepherd slept all the way home," laughs Serra, who believes this is a trail for hikers in good shape. "It's a beautiful, wooded trail that goes all the way up to the most stunning views of the Litchfield Hills and the Berkshires. It's spectacular. If you want a walk with a view, Bear Mountain is it."

Each winter, head to Jumpfest to see an absolutely thrilling display of athleticism. Ian Johnson

Farmington: Need something to do? Well, just head to **Winding Trails** (**www.windingtrails.org**) for a winter activity when Mother Nature cooperates. This nonprofit on 380 incredible acres of nature's bounty is well-known for its cross-country skiing opportunities. "Should the snow fall, we offer 12.5 miles of groomed trails for both ski-skating and traditional diagonal stride. We have a ski center that offers lessons. We've got 240 sets of rental equipment. We have a lodge with a roaring fire and a small snack bar," says Executive Director Scott Brown. As one of the only places in the state that rents out equipment, it's a really convenient spot for trying out this exhilarating sport, considered a great workout. "Cross-country skiing has been touted as the number-one aerobic exercise; it's a full-body workout, so from a health standpoint it's wonderful. And there's the mental component. You are out in the woods, you are enjoying nature, you can see nature, you're in the outdoors,

Original masterpieces by Claude Monet can be viewed in a home setting at Hill-Stead Museum. Caryn B. Davis Photography

breathing the fresh air, and it's wonderful on all levels," says Brown, noting that most people don't struggle on these trails. "Our most difficult trail here in Farmington, Connecticut, would be considered an easy trail in Vermont or New Hampshire." Winding Trails features a beginner course through the woods, where a skier might just spy a few deer watching quietly from behind a tree. It guides participants up and down hills, which can be challenging on the long and skinny skis. Many folks with developmental disabilities can take part, although there's no special equipment available for those with physical disabilities. Farmington is also home to the incredible **Hill-Stead Museum (www .hillstead.org)**, open year-round. This beautiful home was the maiden project for Theodate Pope Riddle, one of the first licensed female architects in the United States. She was truly a groundbreaking woman of her time. The Colonial Revival mansion, an early twentieth-century country estate with 152 acres of gardens and grounds, became the country home for Riddle's parents and has been open to the public since 1947. But that's not all. "On the inside is the world-class collection of Impressionist art and decorative art, all authentic to the period of the beginning of the twentieth century," says Executive Director Anna Swinbourne, noting that visitors see original works of art by Claude Monet, Edgar Degas, James M. Whistler, Mary Cassatt, and more. The stunning paintings were collected by Riddle's father, Alfred Atmore Pope. Seeing these paintings in a home setting, as opposed to a cavernous museum, is an intimate, unique experience. Winter brings special programming to Hill-Stead. "Once the weather begins to get colder, we move inside, and we begin the season with a series of concerts inside the drawing room of the historic house, which has probably the highest concentration of the Impressionist paintings," says Swinbourne, detailing the home's holiday decorations and festive vibe. Also, on the first weekend in December, there's a multiday holiday boutique with performers and vendors. The first floor of the home, the shop, a gallery, and the Sunken Garden are accessible for those in wheelchairs. There is one wheelchair on-site available for borrowing.

Winsted/Winchester: Walk through the doors of an old mill building in Winsted and be wowed. The **American Mural Project** (**www.american muralproject.org**), founded by the incredible Ellen Griesedieck, is believed to be the largest indoor collaborative piece of artwork in the

The American Mural Project is a giant work of art that showcases the professions that make our world go around. Peter Brown Architectural Photography

world, measuring 120 feet long and five stories tall. Griesedieck, a veteran artist and photographer, came up with this grand idea in 2001. While it took twenty years to reach fruition and be open to the public, it is now a sight to behold. Colorful and full of different materials, like marble, steel, blown glass, and even kelp from Maine, it shows the American Dream with visual vignettes based on real-life characters, like Eddie the truck driver. From farms to factories, Griesedieck traveled the country, meeting all those featured in the massive mural. She tells their unique tales through art. In addition, she met with thousands of schoolchildren from all around the United States, working their unique creations into the work of art. "It's a vehicle to inspire. People come in and find themselves in the mural," says Griesedieck. "It has a universality in the message being delivered that touches everyone." Seeing the piece should really be considered an "experience," as folks can gaze upon it from many angles, on two levels, and see something new every time. This is a great activity for all family members—young, old, and of all abilities. "It's all about inclusion," says Griesedieck, noting that getting into the exhibit is easy for those in a wheelchair. There's also an elevator to bring those with mobility issues to the second floor. Winsted is also home to the

American Museum of Tort Law (**www.tortmuseum.org**), founded by American political activist Ralph Nader. It's the first of its kind, meant to inform, educate, and inspire the American public about the trial by jury system. It's open by appointment in the winter and is ADA compliant. Winsted is part of Winchester, considered the Gateway to the Berkshire Mountains. Beautiful **Platt Hill State Park** (**portal.ct.gov/DEEP/State -Parks/Locate-Park-Forest/Other-State-Parks-and-Forests#PlattHill features**) offers great views along with hiking and birding. In addition, there's a moving sight at **Soldiers' Monument & Memorial Park** (**www .soldiersmonumentwinsted.org**), a Gothic Revival–style statue that honors all who have served our country.

Hartford: Winter is a great time to take in all the culture the capital city has to offer thanks to its amazing museums. And what name almost immediately comes to mind when you think of Hartford? Mark Twain, of course. The **Mark Twain House & Museum** (**www.marktwainhouse.org**) is a spacious, lovely home in the Asylum Hill neighborhood where the groundbreaking author of *Huckleberry Finn* lived from 1874 to 1891. His actual name was Samuel Clemons, and during his time in this twenty-five-room house, he wrote *The Adventures of Tom Sawyer*. The first floor of the home is accessible for wheelchairs. Next door, find the **Harriet Beecher Stowe Center** (**www.harrietbeecherstowecenter.org**), which includes the home of the groundbreaking author of the antislavery novel *Uncle Tom's Cabin*, the only international bestseller of the nineteenth century. "We are wonderful neighbors," says Executive Director Karen Fisk, noting that this is a testament to the fact that Twain and Stowe were friends and lived side by side. They shared an affinity for good jokes and social justice. "We are very intent on helping inspire individuals to act in responsible ways, to do something," says Fisk. "The reason to come here is to be inspired to have some hope that no matter what is going on, we as individuals can make a difference." The center's old buildings are not fully accessible, but wheelchairs are accommodated on the first floor. The center also offers an American Sign Language (ASL) tour of four rooms. Next to Stowe's home is the Katherine Seymour Day House, a striking stone structure that belonged to Stowe's grandniece, who started a foundation that eventually led to the creation of the center. Today this stately home serves as the office and research library for the center. View incredible masterpieces at the **Wadsworth Atheneum Museum of Art** (**www.thewadsworth.org**). Founded in 1842, it is considered the oldest

Left: Visit the Stowe Center, including the home of Harriet Beecher Stowe, for a lesson in bravery that resonates today. Right: Next door to the Stowe Center is the Mark Twain House, home of the legendary author.

continually operating public art museum in the country. It now sports more than fifty thousand works of art housed in a unique building that resembles a castle. Find contemporary works by artists such as Andy Warhol, whose painting of Jacqueline Kennedy Onassis is on display, along with pieces by Connecticut's own Sol LeWitt, creator of one-of-a-kind brightly striped murals. Also see classic European pieces by Claude Monet and Pierre-Auguste Renoir. The museum includes a "Sculpture in the City" section, Egyptian bronzes, and even a Colt firearms collection, a nod to Hartford's history with the company. The museum is accessible for those with mobility issues and offers wheelchairs, available on a first-come, first-served basis. The museum also offers an ASL video tour. The kids will absolutely love the **Connecticut Science Center** (**www.ct sciencecenter.org**). Opened in 2009, it's a 154,000-square-foot space that folks of all ages can explore for hours. Built in a state-of-the-art facility in the city's Adrien's Landing section, it features 165 hands-on exhibits, a 3D digital theater, educational labs, a butterfly encounter, STEM learning, and special programs. Small kids will love a first-floor water and bubble emporium, while older kids can present a weather report or stand inside a hurricane simulator booth. The center is ADA compliant, with elevators and some wheelchairs available on-site. It also frequently offers sensory-friendly days for kids on the autism spectrum. Look for cool traveling exhibits, like *Jurassic Quest* or *Beyond Van Gogh*, at the nearby **Connecticut Convention Center** (**www.ctconventions.com**). There's an old-school carousel in the city's Bushnell Park, which affords great walking opportunities. **Connecticut's Old State House** (**wp.cga.ct.gov/osh/**) is a fascinating place—it was home to all three branches of state government from 1796 to 1878. The start of the *Amistad* trial happened in this National Historic Landmark. This ADA-compliant location is very kid-friendly, with

Left: Take to the ice at Winterfest in Hartford! Right: Kids can both play and learn history at Connecticut's Old State House.

areas where youngsters can play but also learn. Lastly, for perfect cold-weather fun, head to **Winterfest (www.winterfesthartford.com)** in **Bushnell Park (www.bushnellpark.org)**, featuring a fantastic skating rink. Believe it or not, skating, skate rentals, and even skating lessons are completely free.

West Hartford: This popular place, right outside the city of Hartford, is probably best known for its bustling downtown area. "It is, first of all, aesthetically beautiful, and it does have a great mix of shopping and restaurants, practically any cuisine you would want, from seafood to burgers to Mediterranean, Mexican, Asian; you name it, we have it in the center," says Chris Conway, president and CEO of the **West Hartford Chamber of Commerce (www.whchamber.com)**, noting the addition of **Blue Back Square (www.bluebacksquare.com)** in 2008, a 250,000-square-foot space filled with shops, restaurants, apartments, and office spaces. He also points out other unique spots in town outside the downtown area. "We actually have five distinct areas of town that also have

their own unique characteristics. We have Bishop's Corner, the Elmwood section, the Park Road section and the New Park Corridor," he says, encouraging folks to get to know the unique vibe of each neighborhood. Also be sure to check out the **Noah Webster House and West Hartford Historical Society (www.noahwebsterhouse**

Visit the Noah Webster House to learn about this American hero who wrote the first American dictionary.

.org). This is where Webster spent his childhood years. Called an "American hero," Webster wrote textbooks, aiming to revolutionize the education system in the late 1700s. This strong supporter of the American Revolution, and contemporary of Alexander Hamilton, George Washington, and Benjamin Franklin, wrote his first dictionary in 1806. The modest home shows his roots. "It's a great facility and historic landmark that we're proud to have," says Conway. "Noah Webster was more than just the guy who wrote the dictionary. He was an intellectual of his day." Admission to the museum, which is partially wheelchair accessible, is free. For

Blue Back Square has become a hot spot for walking, shopping, and dining.

outdoor recreation, head over to the 3.8-mile loop trail around the **West Hartford Reservoir (www.themdc.org/reservoirs/)**. The **Troutbrook Trail (www.westhartfordct.gov/town-departments/leisure-services/ outdoor-recreation/walking-trails)** is also fantastic for runners, walkers, and bikers. The wide and lengthy trail is accessible for all revelers.

Ledyard: This town, named for a Revolutionary War officer, is probably best known as the home of **Foxwoods Resort Casino (www.foxwoods .com)**, a sprawling, glittery mecca of entertainment that introduced Connecticut to the casino world when it opened in 1997. Find musical and theatrical shows, great restaurants, and even an outlet mall. In winter, Foxwoods boasts a really vibrant area, the Winter Terrace, with a gorgeous ice-skating rink, firepits, and igloos, ready for dining. I've taken the boys there several times, and we've always had a blast. The nine-million-square-foot property, which includes six casinos and a hotel, is owned and operated by the Mashantucket Pequot Tribal Nation. "We look at it as a business venture, not what makes us who we are. The museum is who we are," says Robert Hayward, director of marketing at the nearby **Mashantucket Pequot Museum and Research Center (www.pequot museum.org)**, a state-of-the-art facility. "We are the world's largest Native American museum that is dedicated primarily to the history and culture

See an incredible re-creation of a sixteenth-century Pequot village in Ledyard. Mashantucket Pequot Museum and Research Center

of the Mashantucket Pequot tribe." Aesthetically, the museum is striking, with fascinating exhibits that take visitors on a journey through time. "We go all the way back to the ice age and work our way to modern day, which is very cool," says Hayward. Folks experience the sounds of a glacier, breaking ice, and brisk winds. They even see the re-creation of a giant woolly mammoth. Visitors are always struck by an enormous room, like none other I've ever seen. "It's a twenty-two-thousand-square-foot re-creation of a sixteenth-century Pequot village. It's a favorite spot for everybody because it puts you back in that time," says Hayward. See men out for a hunt and women cooking outside a wigwam in traditional clothing. Audio tours are available. A trip includes an elevator ride to the Observation Tower, giving visitors an awesome view of the reservation and region, with views all the way to the shores of Mystic on a clear day. The museum also hosts public educational powwows to introduce visitors to traditional song and dance. The Museum and Research Center is accessible to all visitors.

Waterbury: The Brass City provides some wonderful culture year-round, but the **Mattatuck Museum** (**www.mattmuseum.org**) is a great place to while away the hours in warmth in the wintertime. The wheelchair-accessible museum collects and shows American art, with a focus on the history of the Naugatuck Valley. "We were started in 1877 as the Mattatuck

Historical Society by a group of founding fathers who wanted to create an institution to share the wealth of information about the history of Waterbury and the greater Waterbury region," explains Executive Director Robert Burns. Housed since 1986 in a former Masonic temple, the museum recently underwent a major nine-million-dollar renovation, reopening to the public in 2021. It offers special programming for children with special needs. "Our art collection, which boasts paintings, sculptures, works on paper, prints, watercolors, photographs, and art photography, is primarily focused on the artists who are from or have lived and worked in the state of Connecticut," explains Burns. "We're also collecting contemporary art and really exhibiting art from all around the world, because we're trying to reflect the diversity of the people of Waterbury." Burns notes the huge influence that people from other countries have had on the city. "Waterbury is a city of many different immigrants from many different places, and our exhibition schedule and our exhibits are

Winter is a great time to explore Waterbury's Mattatuck Museum, with its focus on locally grown artists.
Bradford Mahler

being driven by that," he says. Keeping with that theme, after a visit to the museum, Burns suggests grabbing lunch at one of the city's exceptional restaurants featuring food from all around the world—Italy, Mexico, and Afghanistan, for example. Then make a stop at the **Palace Theater** (**www.palacetheaterct.org**), on the National Register of Historic Places. Built in the early 1920s, with grand touches such as gold trim and crystal chandeliers, the Palace Theater was integral to the local cultural scene before World War II and after, boasting acts such as Harry Houdini, Bing Crosby, and the Glenn Miller Orchestra. But the famous theater started to deteriorate during the 1980s and faced threats of demolition. The theater was dark for fifteen years. In 2000 the city took control of the property, and a thirty-million-dollar restoration and expansion project began. The theater reopened in 2004 with a performance by the legendary Tony Bennett. Today it is home to the hottest Broadway musicals and concerts. "It's a beautiful treasure house that's open to the public for tours and visits, as well as the amazing array of shows they do," says Burns. The theater offers wheelchair accessibility, sensory-friendly performances, assistive-listening devices, and open-captioned performances with a text display of lyrics and dialogue. Finish up a day trip to Waterbury with a stop at **Fascia's Chocolates** (**www.faschoc.com**), where you can make your own candy bar. This location is ADA compliant. (Learn more about Connecticut's Chocolate Trail in the "Unique Outings for Winter" section.)

Southbury: You don't have to travel to the shoreline to see incredible bald eagles. There's a spot in Southbury where they've become plentiful. The **Shepaug Bald Eagle Observation Area** (**www.facebook.com/baldeagles**) on the Housatonic River is open each year from mid-December to early March. FirstLight, a power company, owns and operates

this unique spot that includes a dam. The water around the hydroelectric power station never completely freezes, making it an ideal spot for wintering eagles. And now the area doesn't just see cold-weather visitors. A number of nesting eagles make this beautiful spot their home. The resurgence and recovery of the eagle is really a success story. While they are still threatened and protected, they are

The Shepaug Bald Eagle Observation Area is a great place to view bald eagles in wintertime. Richard Stone

no longer endangered, thanks to environmental and conservation efforts. Bird lovers flock to the observation deck to use scopes or binoculars to view immature or mature eagles soaring, swooping, or perching in trees. "It's almost a spiritual event for people to see them for the very first time," says site manager Lucy Walker. "It is the symbol of our country. It represents freedom. It is a success story. We almost lost this bird, and to be able to see such a beautiful species in the wild is amazing for people." Walker also believes that Connecticut stands out in terms of giving the public a special experience in viewing bald eagles. "Shepaug is certainly unique; I don't think there's another location like Shepaug," she says. Organizers say it's always cold in Southbury, so be sure to wear winter clothes. This excursion is free but does require a reservation. The observation area is wheelchair accessible. Find scenic waterfalls and a covered bridge at **Southford Falls State Park** (**portal.ct.gov/DEEP/State-Parks/Parks/Southford-Falls-State-Park**), former site of the Diamond March Company. This is a great spot for cross-country skiing, hiking, and ice-skating.

Wallingford: This diverse town offers beautiful vistas and hikes during the offseason. Ray Andrewsen of the **Quinnipiac Chamber of Commerce (www.quinncham.com)** suggests that wanderers check out the campus of **Choate Rosemary Hall (www.choate.edu)**, a private high school attended by President John F. Kennedy. "The grounds are beautiful. They are walkable; there's a lot of history there," he says, noting that exploration should lead visitors to the town center. "The downtown area of Wallingford is architecturally diverse and unique." Be sure to see the recently renovated **Nehemiah Royce House (www.wallingford cthistory.org/royce-house)**, a charming white saltbox that is the

Take a walk around Choate Rosemary Hall, the prestigious private high school attended by President John F. Kennedy.

oldest home in town, dating back to 1672. Nearby, find the **American Silver Museum**, housed in the Franklin Johnson Mansion (**www .wallingfordcthistory.org**), a restored Italianate mansion on the National Register of Historic Places. Learn the importance of the silver industry in Wallingford and neighboring towns by viewing a large collection. It's best to call ahead to both locations if wheelchair accessibility is required. The Johnson Mansion sports a wheelchair lift, which allows visitors to see

Left: Check out the Nehemiah Royce House, the oldest home in Wallingford. Right: The expansive views from Gouveia Vineyards are lovely during any season.

the first floor of the museum. The Royce House doesn't offer a ramp, but the entrance to the house is near the ground, and folks in wheelchairs have been assisted in to see the first floor. Additionally, full online tours are available on the website. This town has an interesting blend of agricultural and manufacturing aspects. "Wallingford does have the only steel plant in the state, Nucor Steel Connecticut," says Andrewsen. "The east side of Wallingford is much like Vermont; it has that feel to it. The views from **Gouveia Vineyards** (**www.gouveiavineyards.com**) are outstanding," he says. "You can see for miles and miles. It has become a favorite destination for many people." Allison Gouveia Gatcomb, whose parents opened the vineyard in 2003, says visitors come from all around, even outside New England. "Our sunsets are well known, and they're quite beautiful," she says. "It's a family business, and it's amazing how big we've grown." The sunny vineyard grows a nice variety of whites, reds, and of course a refreshing rosé. This location is ADA compliant. (For more about this vineyard, check out the "Unique Outings for Fall" section.)

Durham: This rural town, located halfway between Hartford and New Haven, may as well be dubbed Christmas Tree-ville! Make the trip to Durham to find that perfect Tannenbaum! For many families, strolling through the fields in the crisp air—talking and laughing while searching for the perfect tree—is a beloved tradition. Cut down the perfect pick at **Miller Tree Farm, Dumas Tree Farm**, or **Herzig Family Tree Farm** (**www.ctchristmastree.org**). "If you think about it, it makes a lot of sense. We have a lot of open space," says Laura Francis, a former town clerk and first selectwoman who has lived in town since 1991. She says the

Left: Durham Town Green is surrounded by historic homes and buildings. Right: In Durham, see the historic Sabbath Day House, where people would rest between church services in the 1800s.

town's history revolves around agriculture and farming. To that end, she suggests checking out a unique building in town called the **Sabbath Day House**, run by the **Durham Historical Society** (**www.townofdurhamct .org**). "Back in the day, church would be an all-day event, so there would be these little structures on the Town Green

Next to the Sabbath Day House, find the Old Center School, built in 1775.

to give people a place to rest between services." Very close by, find the **Old Center School**, built in 1775. Both structures, open to the public periodically, are situated next to Durham's lovely Town Green, where anyone can pass by and gaze upon them. Also make a stop at **Tri-Mountain State Park (portal.ct.gov/DEEP/State-Parks/Locate -Park-Forest/Other-State-Parks-and-Forests#TriMountain)** or **Millers Pond State Park (portal.ct.gov/DEEP/State-Parks/Parks/Millers-Pond -State-Park)** in **Cockaponset State Forest (portal.ct.gov/DEEP/State -Parks/Forests/Cockaponset-State-Forest)**, both great spots for hiking. Take note of the bronze markers in town, informing visitors that George Washington passed through Durham in 1775.

East Haven: The Big Guy in Red is no stranger to the **Shore Line Trolley Museum (www.shorelinetrolley.org)**, bringing magic to the station every Christmas! "We've been doing it for so long. For over thirty years, Santa has been visiting the Shore Line Trolley Museum," says Executive Director John Proto. "It's really cool when you see people who say they've been coming here and brought their kids, and now they're bringing their grandkids. It's really turned into a local tradition for a lot of people." A visit includes a ride on an old-fashioned trolley and gifts for little boys and girls. The museum operates the Branford Electric Railway, which dates back to the 1900s, making it the oldest continuously operated trolley line in the country, as recognized by the US Department of the Interior. The site, which celebrates the Golden Age of Transportation, is listed on the National Register of Historic Places. "I look at it as a history museum. Most of what we have is over one hundred years old," says Proto. "We have one of the only surviving cable cars from the San Francisco 1906 earthquake." The museum's collection also includes trolleys from

Get in the holiday spirit when Santa visits the Shore Line Trolley Museum each Christmas. Michael Gambino

New York, Canada, New Orleans, and the oldest known horse-drawn streetcar in existence, which ran in Central Park in 1860. The museum recently received a grant to purchase chairlifts to get those with mobility issues into the trolleys. Additionally, there are plans to make pathways even more accessible. Looking for ice-skating opportunities, even if Mother Nature doesn't cooperate? Head to the Pasquale G. **"Patsy" DiLungo Veterans Memorial Ice Rink** (**www.easthaven-ct.gov**), revamped in 2022 and named for a local businessman who was very active in the youth hockey scene. Home to figure-skating lessons and ice hockey leagues, it also offers skating for the public. Skate rentals are available. **Farm River State Park** (**portal.ct.gov/DEEP/State-Parks/Parks/Farm-River-State-Park**) is a great spot for a winter hike by the sparkling water.

UNIQUE OUTINGS FOR WINTER

During Valentine's season, be sure to check out **Connecticut's Chocolate Trail** (***www.ctvisit .com/trail/chocolate***), a concept cooked up by the state's tourism department as a fun way to explore the area. The trail consists of about twenty locations, including **Divine Treasures** (***www.dtchocolates.com***) in Manchester, with a decadent selection of organic European dark chocolate. Move over to West Hartford Center to sample the European classics at **Bridgewater Chocolate** (***www.bridgewaterchocolate.com***), offering luxurious sweet treats since 1995. Famous **Munson's Chocolates** (***www.munsonschocolates.com***) is well represented in the

state with ten locations, including the Bolton headquarters, Farmington, and Glastonbury. Head to Meriden for a tasty trip to **Thompson Chocolate** (***www .thompsonchocolate.com***), open since 1879. Not far away, find **Tschudin Chocolates & Confections** (***www .tschocolates.com***), a fun shop in downtown Middletown featuring such humorous designs as chocolate pianos, sky-high edible stilettos, and magical "mermaid lions." To the west, **Waterbury's Fascia's Chocolates** (***www.faschoc.com***) sports a one-thousand-square-foot space where visitors can make their own candy

Find decadent treats from Waterbury to Old Lyme along Connecticut's Chocolate Trail.

bar. This popular destination is known for its chocolate-dipped pretzels and a boxed assortment of various chocolates, filled with fruity or nutty fillings. The trail continues into the Litchfield Hills with a stop at **Thorncrest Farm & Milk House Chocolates** (***www.milkhousechocolates .net***) in Goshen. The delicious journey continues down on the shoreline at the **Chocolate Shell** (***www.thechocolateshell.com***), called "the sweetest destination in Old Lyme" since 1980.

There's just something about taking an old-fashioned sleigh ride through the fresh snow, accompanied by jingle bells, that brings you right into the lyrics of a Christmas carol. Dash through the snow at **Allegra Farm** (***www.allegrafarm.com***) in East Haddam, a beautiful place run by a true original. John Allegra wants to take folks back in time as he settles them under some cozy blankets and zooms them around the grounds of his twenty-acre property. "A lot of people have the dream of checking a sleigh ride off their bucket list. We're one of the only outfits left, if Mother Nature cooperates, that do it in an authentic sleigh with a pair of horses, over the brook and through the woods to Grandma's house," he says with a twinkle in his eye. He has provided antique vehicles like sleighs and carriages for movies such as The Greatest Showman and Little Women.

Go dashing through the snow at Allegra Farm in East Haddam!

Another magical activity? Take the kids to a gingerbread house class at the **Silo Cooking School at Hunt Hill Farm**. (See "New Milford" in the "Spring" section for more information.) Master house maker Nancy Stuart starts shopping for candy right after Halloween. She walks participants through making homemade dough. Once the dough is baked, the action moves to an enormous table filled with dozens of candy toppings. Participants don't feel pressured to make the perfect house. It's all about bonding with tablemates and creating a house with charm and character. The school has recently been renovated to create increased accessibility for all.

Nancy Stuart shows a student how to make the perfect gingerbread house at Hunt Hill Farm.

Essex doesn't have a lock on the toy train game. You can also head to the lovely hamlet of Wilton to discover mini locomotives at Christmastime. Every year, the **Wilton Historical Society (www.wilton historical.org)** hosts the Great Trains Holiday Show from Thanksgiving through mid-January. The halls are decked in the society's antique buildings, complete with model trains chugging through small, scenic vistas. The society also offers holiday concerts, open-hearth cooking demonstrations, and visits with Santa.

See the Great Trains Holiday Show at the Wilton Historical Society. Nick Foster

Nothing says "holiday" like a drive or stroll through a light show! And Connecticut boasts some great ones. Be sure to check out **Hebron Lights in Motion (www.lionslightsinmotion.org)**, the **Reed Family Light Show (www.facebook.com/reedfamilylightshow/)**; the **Festival of Silver Lights (www.meridenct.gov/community-events/2018/01/01/festival-of-silver-lights/)** in Meriden's Hubbard Park; **Fantasy of Lights (www.goodwillsne.org/fantasyoflights/)** in New Haven; and **Ivoryton Illuminations (www.ivorytonalliance.org/2022-illuminations-info)**. There are also great displays at **Lake Compounce (www.lakecompounce.com)** and **Olde Mistick Village (www.oldemistickvillage.com)**.

Don't miss three other uniquely Connecticut winter events. **Carl Bozenski's Christmas Village** *(torringtonct.myrec.com/info/facilities/details.aspx?FacilityID=14725)* in Torrington has been a holiday tradition since 1947. Kids can enjoy a cup of cocoa before or after a spirited visit with Santa, Mrs. Claus, and the elves. Also check out the Lantern Light Village at **Mystic Seaport Museum** *(www.mysticseaport.org)*, basically a walking play set on Christmas Eve in 1876. A touching story is woven throughout the village as visitors stroll past the historic buildings and ships. "It's a special time, and it's very well done. The setting here is perfect, and you feel transformed back in time. It's very immersive," says Sophia Matsas, the museum's director of marketing and communications. Take the kids to see a real-life reindeer at **Dzen Tree Farm** *(www.dzentreefarm.com)* in South Windsor. They'll be delighted, I promise. And see the incredible artist palettes, mini-masterpieces that adorn the holiday trees at the **Florence Griswold Museum** *(www.florencegriswoldmuseum.org)*.

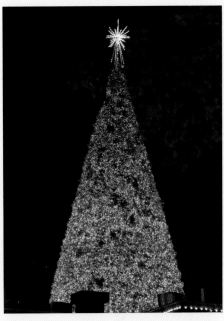

Every year, Lake Compounce gets all dressed up for the holidays with a beautiful light display. Lake Compounce

Left: The Florence Griswold Museum in Old Lyme displays more than two hundred artist palettes on gorgeous trees during the holidays. Top right: Find holiday magic with nautical charm during the Lantern Light Village tours at Mystic Seaport Museum. Mystic Seaport Museum. Bottom right: Each holiday season, children love to see the reindeer at Dzen Tree Farm in South Windsor.

See spring in bloom at Preston's Wicked Tulips.

Spring

We all know that feeling. The feeling of those first warm days of spring. There's that smell in the air as the birds chirp at a different velocity. When spring hits Connecticut, folks are out, and I mean OUT, walking the dogs, strolling the beach, taking the kids to the playground. And when fields turn yellow with vibrant daffodils and Easter hats emerge from dusty closets, we know we're in the clear. Enjoy these stops that will make your spring just a little brighter!

Washington: Washington is said to be the inspiration for the fictional town of Stars Hollow, made famous in my favorite TV series, *Gilmore Girls*. It's known for both its bucolic beauty and rich cultural scene. The town exists on the ancestral homelands of the Weantinock and Pootatuck peoples. The **Institute for American Indian Studies (www.iais museum.org)** tells their important story. This site, known for workshops and special programs, has been open since the 1970s and features a life-size replica of a sixteenth-century Algonkian village. "It's very authentic. Half the adventure is getting there, because you drive on this gorgeous wooded road," explains Connecticut tourism expert Janet Serra. "They do have one of the biggest collections of Native American Woodland Indian artifacts anywhere." In recent years, staff added an innovative and modern aspect to the museum to appeal to a younger demographic. Called the Wigwam Escape Room, the hands-on experience requires a group, perhaps a family, to work together to solve a puzzle that begins in the year 1518. The objective is to gather supplies for a journey. "It's very clever," says Serra. The museum is accessible, as is the outside village, which is best accessed by a four-wheel-drive vehicle. Find peace in nature at **Hollister House Garden (www.hollisterhousegarden.org)**, featuring an American interpretation of an English garden created by antiques dealer George Schoellkopf. "It's a very special garden. It's a public garden, but it's a very personal garden," says Executive Director Pamela Moffett. Find gorgeous plants and flowers in the garden's defined spaces, referred to as "rooms," which are separated by tall walls, hedges, and even different

Find true peace and natural beauty at Hollister House Garden in Washington.

levels. This beauty is framed by a winding brook, a large pond, and even a woodland path. The garden scene doesn't stop there. Visit the **Judy Black Memorial Park & Gardens (www.thejudyblackparkandgardens.org)**, meant to be a relaxing gathering place for families and friends. **Mount Bushnell State Park** offers great hiking opportunities around Lake Waramaug, as does the **Steep Rock Preserve (www.steeprockassoc .org/preserve/steep-rock/)**, with almost one thousand acres, including wooded hills and river views. "Washington is a lovely small town that has really retained the feeling of a New England country town," says Moffett, noting that folks often complement a visit here with a stop in nearby Litchfield. There is limited accessibility at the Hollister House Garden.

Kent: Nearby Washington and nestled into the northwest corner of the state, this lovely town features a fascinating mix of history and rural charm. Plus, there's a plethora of museums to explore. Let's begin at **Kent Falls State Park (portal.ct.gov/DEEP/State-Parks/Parks/Kent -Falls-State-Park)**. "It's beautiful; I love Kent Falls," says Janet Serra, who was a tourism director for thirty-five years in both the Litchfield Hills and Fairfield County. This area features a series of waterfalls. The flow of the falls is particularly dramatic in spring, when the snow is melting and the weather is changing. Also in Kent, find one of the state's nine covered bridges. **Bulls Bridge**, listed on the National Register of Historic Places, stretches over the Housatonic River and is considered one of three historically significant bridges in the state. In fact, it is home to a well-known tale. "It was rumored that George Washington's horse fell into the Housatonic," says Serra. **Macedonia State Park** is also a great spot for hiking (**portal.ct .gov/DEEP/State-Parks/Parks/ Macedonia-Brook-State-Park**). The **Eric Sloane Museum** (**www .ericsloane.com/museum**) teaches visitors about the well-known author and illustrator of more than thirty books, including *A Reverence for Wood*.

Visit the Eric Sloane Museum, on the National Register of Historic Places. Lynn M. Worthington

The museum and gift shop are fully accessible. Listed on the National Register of Historic Places, it's quite a unique spot. Folks can see the remains of the Kent Iron Furnace, which operated from 1826 to 1892 on the property, Sloane's replica of an early 1800s pioneer cabin, and an impressive collection of historic tools. Across the street, the **Connecticut Antique Machinery Association** (**www.ctamachinery.com**) is a wheelchair-accessible museum dedicated to preserving and showcasing antique machinery such as tractors. The eight-acre grounds include a narrow-gage railroad. Every April the museum hosts a Spring Power-Up and Open House to christen the new season. This location also includes a **Mining Museum**. "It's a hidden gem, no pun intended," says Serra.

Left: See beautiful Bulls Bridge, a charming covered bridge stretching over the Housatonic River in Kent. Don Hicks. Right: Kent Falls are particularly dramatic during the spring. Kent Chamber of Commerce

Middletown: In springtime, a beautiful mansion that elicits thoughts of Downton Abbey comes alive with color and activity. "Since we are a city-owned building, we try to offer free public events to the community as much as possible. Usually that starts with our Daffodil Days in April," explains Megan Busch, executive director of the beautiful **Wadsworth Mansion (www.wadsworthmansion.com)**, surrounded by over one hundred acres of wooded parklands. Daffodil Days include a look at some gorgeous flowers, live music, historical tours, food trucks, hiking on trails,

Wadsworth Mansion in Middletown hosts Daffodil Days, special events during springtime. Wadsworth Mansion

and kids' activities, held both inside and outdoors. The mansion hosts weddings and private get-togethers, which enable organizers to fund the public events. The home's history is fascinating. "It was built in the early 1900s by Colonel Clarence Wadsworth for his wife, Katharine Hubbard, who was from a local family. They wanted a summer home that was based on the French country estates," says Busch. The colonel was a distant cousin of the man who founded the Wadsworth Atheneum Museum in Hartford. After his death, part of the land was willed to the state and became **Wadsworth Falls State Park (portal.ct.gov/DEEP/State-Parks/Parks/Wadsworth-Falls-State-Park)**. Today, it is still a popular spot for hiking and outdoor recreation. The mansion became a religious retreat called the Cenacle. But in the 1980s it became vacant and fell into disrepair. The city purchased the property, which was revitalized in part by private citizens. Now it is a vibrant place, welcoming the public from spring through the fall. The summertime Music at the Mansion series brings thousands of people to the lawn to listen to local acts. Also explore an open-air market with one hundred vendors. The mansion is accessible for all, and the grounds are fairly flat. Children ages one to seven will love to explore **Kidcity Children's Museum (www.kid citymuseum.com)**. Located downtown, it features themed rooms where adults and little ones can engage in pretend play together. My boys loved this special place. This location features an elevator, ADA-compliant restrooms, and quiet spots for those with sensory issues. Speaking of the historic downtown area, which also includes **Wesleyan University**,

Middletown boasts a vibrant main street filled with great restaurants and shops like **Amatos (www.amatosmiddletown.com)**, the kind of classic hobby shop you don't see much anymore.

Stratford: There's so much aviation history in Connecticut, and a fairly new location, opened in May 2021, aims to share it with the public. The **Connecticut Air & Space Center (www.ctairandspace.org)** is housed inside a large hangar. The museum has three main sections, one detailing the life of Gustave Whitehead, who may have flown before the Wright

Brothers in 1901. He was from Germany and lived in Bridgeport. "We also celebrate Igor Sikorsky. He came to Connecticut in 1929 and built his factory across the street from where we are," says Len Roberto, on the museum's board of directors. Sikorsky developed the first ocean-crossing flying boats in the 1930s. Roberto says the museum also teaches visitors about production

See a Sikorsky Memorial Corsair at the Connecticut Air & Space Center in Stratford. Leonard J. Roberto Jr.

during World War II. "The Corsair fighter plane was developed and built in Stratford. The engines were built in Connecticut. The propellers were built in Connecticut. It's the state airplane of Connecticut. Seven thousand were built in the factory right across the street from where our museum is, from 1942 to 1948," explains Roberto. As a nod to Rosie the Riveter, visitors learn how trailblazing women impacted the industry. "We have displays and memorabilia about who they were and what they did, their stories," says Roberto. Many of the aircraft on display, such as the Corsair, are relics saved from disrepair. The center is wheelchair accessible. This visual hangar, jam-packed with interesting nuggets, appeals to everyone from veterans to children. Speaking of veterans, check out the **Stratford Veterans Museum (www.stfdveteransmuseum .org)**, recognizing local servicemen and -women. An important stop is the **Ruby & Calvin Fletcher African American History Museum (www .africanamericanmuseumct.org)**, the state's first destination of its kind. It tells personal stories of people who struggled during the times of slavery and the civil rights movement. The Fletchers collected these artifacts over their lifetime. Admission to this destination is free of charge.

(Donations are gratefully accepted.) The museum is accessible for those in wheelchairs. **Boothe Memorial Park & Museum (www.boothe memorialpark.org)** is set on thirty-two beautiful acres and listed on the National Register of Historic Places. The Boothe Homestead is called the "oldest homestead in America," dating back to 1663. Museum tours are available June through Labor Day. The grounds include interesting buildings, such as a miniature lighthouse and windmill. For the kids, find a playground and farm animals. The first floor of the museum, the clock tower, and the rose garden are all wheelchair accessible.

Guilford: There's a great way to see this gorgeous town, and it's one step up from a stroll! Jump on a high-tech scooter with **Shoreline Segway (www.segwaytoursandrentals.com)** and do some speedy sightseeing with tour guide and owner Richard Petrillo, who gives folks a

Left: Take to the streets of Guilford on a Segway for a tour of town like none other. Right: See farm animals and learn fun facts at bucolic Dudley Farm, filled with history.

comprehensive lesson about staying steady on the wheeled transporter. "The machines are very easy to ride. Most people get acclimated in just a couple of minutes," he says, noting that the six-mile tour begins after the lesson. "We take participants through the historic district of Guilford, across our picturesque green. We go by the Guilford Fairgrounds." Participants roll through neighborhoods then to the beautiful town marina, with classic views of Long Island Sound, tidal wetlands, and an iconic red shack. "I say it's the most painted or photographed building in town," says Petrillo. The tour continues past the **Henry Whitfield State Museum (portal.ct.gov/ECD-HenryWhitfieldStateMuseum)**, the oldest house in Connecticut and the oldest stone house in New England. "It is

This iconic red shack on the coast of Guilford is often painted and photographed.

a really cool place. We enjoy showing it off," says Petrillo. "It's a beautiful ride." This is an adventure for those age fourteen and up. If you're not quite up for a Segway excursion, there are walking tours of this beautiful area, as well. Find information at **Visit Guilford** (**www.visitguilfordct .com**), a great resource that points visitors in the direction of historic barns. **Bishop's Orchards** (**www.bishopsorchards.com**), a fun and vibrant spot year-round, is a great spot for families to pick fresh berries in spring. Pick-your-own season starts in mid-June with strawberries. Channel more of the agricultural spirit at the **Dudley Farm** (**www.dudleyfarm.com**), where folks can take a self-guided walking tour of the farm grounds that includes opportunities to stroll through the bucolic fields. Or tour the historic home from 1845. "We are a late nineteenth-century agricultural museum, the homestead of the Dudley family," says Museum Director Beth Payne of the prosperous farmers who lived here. "We were just accepted on the National Register of Historic Places as the Dudley Farm Historic District. We have ten and a half acres and fifteen buildings, so it's like a mini Old Sturbridge Village." See an organic community garden, along with animals such as chickens and sheep. From spring through summer, the popular farmers' market is bustling every Saturday morning. The museum, inside the homestead, is open June through October and holds a fascinating collection of more than two hundred artifacts, such as arrowheads, from the Dawnland Quinnipiac tribe. "Our barn is actually three barns that are interconnected, and it's on the Connecticut Barn Trail (see sidebar for more information)," says Payne of additional places to explore. Due to the historic nature of this property, it is not wheelchair accessible. For outdoor recreation, stop by beautiful **Chittenden Park** (**www.visitguilfordct.com/todo/chittenden-park/**), with bocce courts and a boardwalk down to the shore of Long Island Sound, as well as access to the National New England Trail.

Windsor Locks: This town is the home of Bradley International Airport. So it's no surprise that one of its main attractions deals with flight. Walk into the truly impressive **New England Air Museum (www.neam.org)** and be wowed. Three large exhibit hangars are filled with history and inspiration in this facility, the only major air museum in New England.

See fantastic historic aircraft at the New England Air Museum. NEAM

"We have over one hundred beautifully restored historic military and civilian aircraft," says President and CEO Stephanie Abrams, pointing out special planes such as the Boeing B-29 Superfortress and the Lockheed 10-A Electra. "Our exhibits aren't just lifeless machines; they're a window into humanity's fascination with flight and our relentless drive to reach new heights." This museum, which features flight simulators and open cockpits, truly appeals to visitors of any age, from toddlers to senior citizens. New exhibits

The New England Air Museum recently debuted a groundbreaking exhibit about the famed Tuskegee Airmen. NEAM

detail women in aviation, along with the famed Tuskegee Airmen, the African American trailblazers who fought in World War II while also battling racism. "The Tuskegee Airmen changed the world and, by keeping their story alive, they continue to do so," says Abrams. "Our goal is not simply to preserve the past but to inspire greatness and change for the future." The museum is accessible, with wheelchairs on-site and large walkways that are easy to navigate. On the Connecticut Fire Academy grounds, see the **Connecticut Firefighters Memorial (portal.ct.gov/ CFPC/content/Fallen-Firefighters-Memorial)**, a monument with an eternal flame honoring nearly 350 local heroes who died in the line of duty. Located near the Connecticut River, Windsor Locks got its name due to a pair of canal locks that opened in 1829. Head to **Windsor Locks Canal State Park (portal.ct.gov/DEEP/State-Parks/Parks/Windsor -Locks-Canal-State-Park-Trail)**, with a 4.5-mile bike and walking trail that overlooks the Connecticut River and old canal.

New Britain: This urban area, known as the Hardware City, has deep manufacturing roots, as it was home to Stanley Works, maker of tools. The **New Britain Industrial Museum (www.nbindustrial.org)**, accessible for all, details this important history with artifacts that represent more than two hundred years of invention in the area. Today the city is also known as an artistic destination. To visit the **New Britain Museum of American Art (www.nbmaa.org)**, make online reservations or simply walk into the peaceful galleries, filled with fascinating works. "One of the things this museum is most proud of is illuminating the voices of underrepresented American artists and ensuring that all of our visitors who walk through the door will find something on our walls that reflect their own identity," says Lisa Lappe, director of communication and visitor experience. This museum, founded in 1903, is considered the first museum in the country to show strictly American art. See Impressionist paintings among its collection, now totaling more than 8,300 works of art, including sculptures and photographs. "We have the largest collection of Sol LeWitt prints in the world," says Lappe, referring to the conceptual minimalist artist, famous for his brightly colored graphic works, who was born in Hartford and spent his later years in Chester. The museum, which is ADA accessible with wheelchairs on-site, is located next to one-hundred-acre **Walnut Hill Park**, designed by famed landscape architect Frederick Law Olmsted. "The experience of coming to the museum includes not only a museum visit but a picnic in the park or a walk in

See the work of underrepresented artists at the New Britain Museum of American Art. Defining Studios

the park. It's really a therapeutic experience for people to come and spend a day here because of the accessibility to the park," says Lappe, noting that the mission of the museum is to be accessible to everyone, including children. "We make ourselves as accessible to our neighbors as possible by offering free admission on Saturdays and offering scholarships to New Britain students. We are the city's museum." The museum offers audio tours for those who can't read or are visually impaired, as well as tours in Spanish and Polish. Extended hours on Thursdays accommodate those who work during the day. There is also robust digital programming for those who can't stray far from their homes. NBMAA is part of the Connecticut Art Trail (see sidebar), which includes twenty-two museums. Be sure to head to the **Copernican Observatory & Planetarium (web.ccsu.edu/ astronomy/)** at **Central Connecticut State University (www.ccsu .edu)**, which offers free public planetarium shows and use of telescopes to witness the magical night sky. There is space for wheelchairs. The observation deck is accessible, but visiting the observatory involves taking stairs. A trip to see the **New Britain Bees (www.nbbees.com)** is also a crowd pleaser for baseball fans of any age. This team, a member of the Futures Collegiate Baseball League, lights up New Britain Stadium every spring and summer.

New Milford: The **Silo at Hunt Hill Farm (www.thesilo.org)** is a truly special place, one that has been through downs—and now ups—during the last decade. Well-known musician and composer Skitch Henderson and his wife, Ruth, bought this idyllic country property in 1968 and really enlivened the area with culture. Henderson, a legendary pianist, was the music director and conductor of the New York Pops Orchestra and presided over many incredible performances at Carnegie Hall. He was also the original bandleader for *The Tonight Show*, alongside Steve Allen. Over the years, the Hendersons accumulated more than one hundred acres of farmland and built the Silo Cooking School in 1972, where celebrities like Martha Stewart, Jacques Pepin, and Julia Child have whipped up dishes. The couple also shared memorabilia with the public in a unique museum. After Skitch then Ruth passed away, the Silo shut down due to financial issues. It was nearly sold to developers, who planned to demolish the buildings. But Alessandro Piovezahn stepped in, and the unique site has been offering public programming again since 2020. "I fell in love. This place is unbelievable. We have ten historic buildings. They're on the National Register of Historic Places. The main house at the farm was built in 1760. It is pre-Revolution, with original posts and beams," he says. "We have the world's most famous Steinway piano ever built as part of the Skitch Henderson Museum. Go into the museum and experience the place where the New York Pops Orchestra was born in 1983 or the art gallery where Andy Warhol and Jean-Michel Basquiat hung their work on the walls." People can also now rent a cottage on the property with an incredible history. "The little cottage is where Frank Sinatra, Liza Minnelli, Tony Bennett, and all the famous friends of Ruth and Skitch would

The Silo at Hunt Hill Farm, once the home of Skitch Henderson, has been reopened and revitalized.

stay when they came to visit the farm," says Piovezahn. Classes at the cooking school, which has recently been updated for accessibility, also have resumed. (See the "Winter" sidebar for more on gingerbread cooking classes at the Silo.) Looking for a special piece of furniture or a unique collectible? Find a trinket or treasure at **Elephant's Trunk Flea Market** (**www.etflea.com**), open every Sunday from April through December. This outdoor spot has been a tradition for many shoppers since 1976. Vendors selling farm-fresh food or vintage items set up shop in the wee hours of the morning. This is no ordinary experience. It's so popular that tickets are required. Get lunch and snacks at on-site food trucks at this always-evolving location. No pets are allowed. New Milford is also home to **Lovers Leap State Park** (**portal.ct.gov/DEEP/State-Parks/ Parks/Lovers-Leap-State-Park**), with awesome hiking trails, a historic iron bridge, and views of the Housatonic River. The park is named for a notorious rock formation where, according to legend, the Pootatuck chief's daughter, Princess Lillinonah, and her lover fell to their deaths in the 1700s.

Mansfield/Storrs: Storrs is a village in the town of Mansfield, and guess what? It's all about Huskies pride! This area revolves around the **University of Connecticut (www.uconn.edu)**, and attending the incredible men's and women's basketball games at Gampel Pavilion is a big pastime for many Nutmeggers. But there's more to the campus than just the sports scene. For a full-circle lesson about where food is from and how it's made, the public can stop at the Kellogg Dairy Center and take a stroll through the barn to see the Jersey and Holstein cows that are milked every day. That milk is taken to a nearby manufacturing plant where delicious ice cream is made. Folks can head to the **UConn Dairy Bar (www.dining.uconn.edu/uconn-dairy-bar/)**, open Wednesday through Sunday, to watch the process through an observation window. This popular spot produces fifty thousand gallons of ice cream a year and offers twenty-six yummy flavors. From food to culture, **UConn's Jorgensen Center (www.jorgensen.uconn.edu)** is a hot spot for the arts, hosting concerts with well-known performers, comedy shows, classical music, and family entertainment. It offers special seating and accessible restrooms. Special accommodations can also be worked out with a phone call. The **Adventure Park at Storrs (www.my adventurepark.com/location/storrs-ct/)** provides an active, fun challenge for families with kids ages seven and up. Play in the trees while tackling 109 unique obstacles and 28 super-fun ziplines on 9 trails. "The parks are all about getting people active and outdoors, having a great time, challenging themselves, bonding, spending time in nature," says Candie Fisher, president of the Outdoor Ventures Group, with six

Find exercise and thrills on the ropes course at the Adventure Park at Storrs.

parks across the country. The trails are color-coded, similar to ski trails, from yellow to double black diamond. Those twelve and up can even try axe throwing in a safe, outdoor environment. Fisher says participants need to be mobile for this activity, but the park has hosted visitors with prosthetics and kids with autism. Families can hire a guide to help. Mansfield proper is home to the state's only three-screen drive-in theater, playing first-run and family films. The **Mansfield Drive-In Theatre & Marketplace (www.mansfielddrivein.com)** offers movies from April through September and a flea market from late March through November on Sundays. This location is ADA compliant. For more outdoor fun, head to **Mansfield Hollow State Park (portal.ct.gov/DEEP/State-Parks/Parks/ Mansfield-Hollow-State-Park)** for boating, fishing, picnicking, and hiking. From late May to mid-October, visit the **Gurleyville Gristmill (www .joshuastrust.org/gurleyville-grist-mill)**, the state's only remaining stone gristmill, dating back to the 1800s. See old-fashioned milling equipment and learn the history of this fascinating site, which was run by the family of Wilbur Cross, a former governor of Connecticut.

Westport: Once home to Paul Newman, Joanne Woodward, Phil Donahue, Marlo Thomas, and Don Imus, Westport is known as a beautiful, swanky town filled with gorgeous vistas and interesting people. My now husband and I bought our first house in Fairfield when we got engaged. I was in heaven, playing "house" and discovering our new surroundings, which would be "home" for seven

The view from Connecticut's 9-11 Living Memorial at Sherwood Island State Park in Westport

years. I discovered **Sherwood Island State Park (portal.ct.gov/DEEP/ State-Parks/Parks/Sherwood-Island-State-Park)** in nearby Westport and literally thought I'd found paradise. Like Hammonasset in Madison, it is truly a magnificent place, where all folks can enjoy the natural beauty that Connecticut has to offer. Sherwood Island is, believe it or not, Connecticut's first state park, comprising more than 235 acres. It features several beautiful beaches where visitors can swim and fish. This park sports wheelchairs that can be borrowed by visitors. This is also the site of Connecticut's **9-11 Living Memorial (portal.ct.gov/DEEP/State-Parks/**

Parks/Sherwood-Island-State-Park/CTs-9-11-Living-Memorial), the state's official monument to local victims of the terror attacks. The twin towers were visible from this coastal area before they were destroyed in the tragic event. The nine-foot-long monument is surrounded by benches and flowers where family members, or anyone, can pay their respects and pause in reflection. **Earthplace** (**www.earthplace.org**)

can also be a place of reflection. "Earthplace started off as a nature center and one of the first nature-based preschools in the entire country. Then it grew from there," says Director of Marketing and Development Sophie Pollmann. The sixty-two-acre nature and wildlife sanctuary offers a variety of trails for families to hike while soaking up nature. "We have educational signage throughout

Experience hiking trails and rehabilitated animals at Earthplace in Westport.

the property," says Pollmann. Inside, see exhibits in a nature museum, along with the Animal Hall. "We have bats, chinchillas, bunnies, parrots, turtles, snakes, cockroaches, and tarantulas. We have an observational beehive, which is really cool," says Pollmann. "The star of the show is the Bird of Prey area. We have Chatty and Cerena, two eagles. We have various owls and red-tailed hawks. They're all rescued animals that can't survive in the wild." My sons were so excited to see the majestic eagles up close, so different from seeing them in the trees while on a cruise. The boys really learned about the eagles' size and strength. The building and one of the nature trails are accessible. Earthplace prides itself on working closely with the special needs community, offering programming for those of all abilities. At the end of the day, make a stop in Westport's bustling downtown, filled with well-known shops and restaurants.

Coventry: This quaint rural town is filled with picturesque countryside vistas and antiques shops in its historic village. A particularly bucolic spot in this town, part of the state's Quiet Corner, is **Round Hill Alpacas** (**www.roundhillalpacasct.com**), providing both a great outing and a window into a larger, important mission. "Our tagline is 'Creating Family Fun.' We love to be a stop on people's Sunday afternoon activities to come by and meet our thirty alpacas," says Cindy Hall, who owns the farm along with her husband, Randy. Visitors, who should make an appointment, can touch and feed these curious animals, who are very trainable and love to take walks. During regular visits and an Open Farm Day every fall, Hall also likes to teach visitors about the alpaca's fleece and how it's developed into yarn and then fabric. Folks of all abilities feel a sense of peace around the animals. "People come here, and all their stress kind of releases. You're around the animals, and they're very therapeutic. It's like you're in this wonderful space where the animals bring out the best in us. It just makes you smile," she says, noting that navigating the farm in a wheelchair is doable but challenging. Hall's adult son,

Sure, it's fun to see the animals at Round Hill Alpacas in Coventry, but they are part of a larger purpose. Round Hill Alpacas

Curt, is on the autism spectrum. The Halls originally bought the alpacas to someday be transferred to CLCC, the Creative Living Community of Connecticut, providing living spaces and employment opportunities for those of all abilities. While the community is still being developed, the CLCC Farm Stand is open, providing vocational training and jobs to neurodiverse adults. "It's a quintessential side-of-the-road, post-and-beam beauty, selling jellies, jams, produce, and so much more. The CLCC Farm Stand purchase makes an impact on CLCC's mission," says Hall. Speaking of fresh food, people come from all over to the **Coventry Farmers' Market (www.coventryfarmersmarket.org)**, open every Sunday from June through October on the grounds of the **Nathan Hale Homestead (ctlandmarks.org/properties/nathan-hale-homestead/)**. One of the largest farmers' markets in the state, this weekly event features a plethora of locally grown and made products. The Nathan Hale Homestead, open from May through October, is the birthplace of Connecticut's state hero, dating back to 1776. This is the only place Hale, who was recruited as one of the country's first spies and hanged by the British during the Revolutionary War, ever called home. The museum, which is ADA compliant, sits on seventeen acres adjoining the fifteen-hundred-acre **Nathan Hale State Forest (portal.ct.gov/DEEP/State-Parks/Locate -Park-Forest/Other-State-Parks-and-Forests#NathanHale**), great for hiking and letterboxing, a fun family activity.

Bridgeport: This city is a transportation hub for the southeastern part of the state, thanks to a train station, a ferry terminal, and several important highways, including I-95, passing through it. And all modes of transport lead visitors to a whole lot of fun at Connecticut's **Beardsley Zoo (www .beardsleyzoo.org**). "We've been around for over one hundred years

See incredible animals like Mexican gray wolves and an Amur tiger at Connecticut's Beardsley Zoo. Jack Bradley

now, and our greatest strength has always been the intimacy we have between our animals, the staff, and our guests," says zoo director Gregg Dancho, noting that the zoo's size allows families to get a close look at some amazing creatures. "We also give good quality of life to the animals. We have some of the most endangered species on the planet." Go to see the Amur leopard, Amur tiger, red panda, two-toed sloth, and red wolves. Dancho says this location, the only accredited zoo in the state, is also known for its conservation efforts, education, and research. It takes about two hours to traverse the zoo, perfect for families with small children, who can also ride the carousel and get something to eat. "Afterwards, you can go into Beardsley Park and relax and maybe play some Frisbee. That makes us very special," says Dancho, who aims to give families the opportunity to unplug and enjoy a traditional experience. The zoo is

ADA compliant, and staff has been trained to work with children with special needs. "We feel that we are a facility for everyone," says Dancho. Also in Bridgeport, find Sacred Heart University's **Discovery Science Center and Planetarium** (**www.discoverymuseum.org**), providing exciting hands-on STEAM experiences. Exhibits include *Science in Flight*, *The Universe and You*, and the *Hall of Space*. The incredible Henry B. du Pont III Planetarium allows folks to see an intergalactic show on a thirty-three-foot diameter dome with a state-of-the-art laser system. The facility is ADA compliant, with ramps and elevators for those using wheelchairs. There's even a "quiet space" on the main level if a child needs a break from activity. Behind the museum, find the **Adventure Park** (**www.my adventurepark.com/location/bridgeport-ct/**), an aerial forest park with 38 zip lines and more than 190 treetop platforms on 14 trails connected by bridges, ladders, and other navigable obstacles amidst five acres of trees. Children as young as five years old can climb. "We really have something for everyone, and it's really fun to watch people progress over their visits," says Candie Fisher, president of the Outdoor Ventures Group, which runs the park. Also find three lanes of axe-throwing opportunities, an activity for those twelve and older. This location, with a companion park in Storrs, opens each year in April.

Stonington: What's not to love about Stonington, a postcard-worthy hamlet, the only Connecticut town directly facing the Atlantic Ocean. It boasts a unique attribute. "It's one of the few spots in Connecticut where you can see all three states in one go," says Aaron Lord, museum manager at the **Lighthouse Museum** (**www.stoningtonhistory.org/visit/ the-lighthouse-museum/**). He's referring to the view from the light tower, which looks over the waters of Connecticut, Rhode Island, and New York. "It's the oldest lighthouse museum in the country. We've been operating since 1927 continuously," he explains, noting that visitors learn the significance of the beacon along with history of the town. "We have a whole exhibit on enslavement in

The Lighthouse Museum in the village of Stonington provides a comprehensive maritime history of the area.

Connecticut. It's mainly focused on a man named Venture Smith, who was enslaved; he freed himself from enslavement and went on a mission to save his family." The unique stone lighthouse, which sees about ten thousand visitors each year between May and October, features two floors of living quarters and a glass floor, giving visitors a cool look down into the original water cistern. "It's quite neat, a highlight for a lot of the youngsters," says Lord. Tickets include a voucher to get into a second museum. "The **Captain Nathaniel B. Palmer House (www.stonington history.org/visit/the-captain-nathaniel-b-palmer-house-museum/**) is a three-story historic house museum, an 1850s mansion. Captain Palmer was the first American to explore Antarctica back in 1820," says Lord.

Left: Continue the learning at the Captain Nathaniel B. Palmer House, home of the first American to explore Antarctica. Right: Take a sip of wine and view the vines at Stonington Vineyards.

Neither location is wheelchair accessible. If you're not in the mood for history, perhaps you'd like a crisp, fresh sip of vino. Head to **Stonington Vineyards (stoningtonvineyards.com**), a boutique farm winery set in a bucolic spot with a quaint, country atmosphere. Visitors can pack a picnic, sit on the lawn, take a tour, and enjoy a tasting. White wines are the specialties. Learn about the "science of wine," along with aging, bottling, and labeling. Make it an afternoon, and travel five minutes down the road to **Saltwater Farm Vineyard (www.saltwaterfarmvineyard .com**), located at a former airport. Runways now serve as aisles of growing grapes, while the hangar, with original woodwork dating back to the 1930s, houses tastings and events. This coastal vineyard sports a chic, urban vibe. It has become an extremely popular spot for weddings and receptions over the past seven years. Both vineyard tasting rooms are accessible for those in wheelchairs. For the adventurous, give **Warbird**

Experience a jingle. "We offer a once-in-a-lifetime experience—to get in a vintage World War II training aircraft," says owner Mark Simmons. "Flying a piece of history is an incredible experience. It's the preservation of a piece of aviation history so the next generation can experience what the greatest generation did to preserve our country. Every flight is unique." This business, in the village of Pawcatuck, offers fifteen- to sixty-minute scenic flights, as well as lessons and charters. Routes show off the Rhode Island and Connecticut coastlines. "It's a beautiful area in the spring and fall, especially with the change of seasons," says Simmons, noting that flights leave from Groton, Connecticut, or Westerly, Rhode Island.

North Stonington: With twenty acres of grapes, **Jonathan Edwards Winery** (**www.jedwardswinery.com**) blends New England charm with Napa Valley style. This beautiful winery, surrounded by gorgeous nature, is one of the largest in the state. Visitors can embark on a tasting and tour of this bicoastal winery that grows grapes in both California and Connecticut, where the weather can be challenging for some varieties. See the oak barrels in a back room, then sample various wines in the tasting room. The goal is to make a high-end wine with Vinifera, a European grape vine. Folks bring a picnic to enjoy on the patio, overlooking rows and rows of vines. Those in wheelchairs can access the tasting room and patio. **Terra Firma Farm** (**www.terrafirmafarm.org**), a nonprofit community farm, invites folks to learn about the importance of local agriculture. "We have a full working dairy and livestock farm; then we offer summer camps, after-school programs, weekend programs, and adult classes immersing the community in the working farm," says owner Brianne Casadei, also known as Farmer Brie. "What makes us different from any of the other farms is we have a processing plant for our dairy. So we milk the cows, and the milk goes right from the cows into the tank. Then we have pasteurizers and bottlers. We make chocolate milk, coffee milk, strawberry milk, cookies-n-cream milk. People come from all over for our milk." The busy farm stand is another example of showing kids and adults the importance of understanding where our food

Visit the Jonathan Edwards Winery, one of the largest vineyards in the state, for a picnic or tasting.

comes from. "We're trying to bring people back to that and give them a moment to see the cows, to see the milk production, to see chicken laying eggs, to connect to the fact that food comes from farms," says Casadei.

East Granby: If you haven't been to this incredibly unique location in East Granby, you need to schedule a visit. We're talking about the **Old Newgate Prison & Copper Mine (portal.ct.gov/DECD/Content/ Historic-Preservation/04_State_Museums/Old-Newgate-Prison-and -Copper-Mine)**. "It's a designated National Historic Landmark and recognized as the first chartered copper mine and first state prison in North America," says curator and site administrator Morgan Bengel, noting that it became a prison in the 1770s. "They used the abandoned mine to house the incarcerated men and eventually built up the infrastructure as they went through the American Revolution and into the early republic, defining what prison was in early America." From May through October every year, visitors can self-guide through the one-acre prison yard with multiple buildings and a twelve-foot-high perimeter wall. Areas are

The grounds of Old Newgate Prison show ruins of old cells, a guard building, and a perimeter wall.

accompanied by fact-filled signage and exhibits. In order to climb down into the copper mine, visitors must sign up for a thirty-minute guided tour, which covers a one-hundred-yard underground loop. "You go as far as seventy-five feet below the surface. It's fifty-two degrees, cold, wet, and dark," says Bengel. "It's unique and authentic. There's nothing like it in our state, let alone the country in terms of a mine turned prison." Speaking from experience, the climb down into this dank, fascinating mine is unlike anything I've ever done. Exhibits are growing and adapting all the time. "We're also trying to make it relevant to modern-day incarceration, so we incorporate voices from formerly incarcerated men and women who are able to shed some light on the modern conditions, how they relate to and differ from the past," says Bengel, explaining that it's an effort to bring humanity to the prisoners. "The site is very romanticized, with escape stories and the American Revolution. It's very easy to get wrapped up in the drama of it, which is fun and great; we're never trying to take that away from people, but there's definitely more to it. These people were inhumanely incarcerated in an abandoned copper mine, so we definitely try to home in on that." But beware. The entire site offers very little accessibility for those with disabilities. Loose-gravel pathways and steep hills make the ruins difficult to navigate, while the

A climb down seventy-five feet underground into a copper mine turned prison is an experience like none other.

climb down into the mine would be nearly impossible. "There are virtual tours of the copper mine and the entire site available on our website," says Bengel. East Granby is also known for natural resources, including rapids on the Farmington River. The **Tariffville Gorge**, accessed through **Cowles Park**, offers hiking and mountain biking opportunities. Folks can also hike the **Metacomet Trail**.

Pomfret: This charming town in what's called Connecticut's Quiet Corner is filled with lovely vistas and rich history. It's perfect for spring exploration. For a dose of nature, check out **Dennis Farm Preserve (www.nature.org/en-us/get-involved/how-to-help/places-we-protect/dennis-farm-preserve)**, a former farm protected by The Nature Conservancy, with a variety of wildlife and interesting plant life. **Mashamoquet Brook State Park (portal.ct.gov/DEEP/State-Parks/Parks/Mashamoquet-Brook-State-Park)** comprises one thousand acres offering camping, fishing, hiking, and great spots for picnicking. This land,

Left: Take a walk around the gorgeous campus at the Pomfret School. Right: Find beauty and history at Mashamoquet State Park.

originally inhabited by the Mohegan tribe, features a famous story from 1742 involving Israel Putnam, who became a well-known general in the Revolutionary War. "Supposedly, he went into the wolf den to pull out a wolf that had been killing a lot of livestock," says John Charest, a member of the **Pomfret Historical Society (www.pomfret-historical-society .org)**. (Learn more about Putnam, and his connection to the town of Brooklyn, in the "Summer" section of this book.) Nearby, find two natural

Left: See antique equipment and tools at Brayton Grist Mill, on the edge of Mashamoquet State Park. Right: Plan a visit to Sharpe Hill Vineyard, a family business that started in New York.

stone formations called Table Rock and Indian Chair. Take time to explore the historic **Brayton Grist Mill & Marcy Blacksmith Museum** on park grounds, which is available for weekend touring, thanks to the Historical Society. "There were a lot of mills built along the Mashamoquet from the beginning of Route 44 near the state park," says Charest. "There was a steep drop in elevation, so they had the ability to turn mill wheels." See antique equipment and blacksmith tools. Charest said there's a lot to enjoy in this tucked-away town: "We love it; it's charming and idyllic. It makes you feel comfortable out here." Also plan a visit to **Sharpe Hill Vineyard (www.sharpehill.com/)**, a family business that started in New York and moved to Connecticut, thanks to a 103-acre parcel of beautiful land. "We bought the property in the summer of 1991," says Jill Vollweiler, noting that it was a labor of love for her mother and father. "We started to plant. It takes five to seven years for the vines to mature, so we opened it to the public in the mid-1990s." Views from the vineyard, set atop a hill, are spectacular, featuring vistas of three different states: Massachusetts, Connecticut, and Rhode Island. The tasting room, which is accessible to those of all abilities, is open during midday hours on Friday, Saturday, and Sunday. Take a stroll around the **Pomfret School** (**www.pomfret.org**). This private high school, founded in 1894, sports a gorgeous campus with sprawling views of the countryside.

Killingly: This town, far away from the hustle and bustle of busy life, is in the state's Quiet Corner as well. It's also within the **Last Green Valley National Heritage Corridor** (**www.nps.gov/places/the-last-green -valley-national-heritage-corridor.htm**), part of the National Park Service, spanning thirty-five towns in northeastern Connecticut and south-central Massachusetts. "The program was started under the Reagan administration back in the '80s," says Assistant Director Francesca Kefalas. "We were formed on November 2, 1994, signed into legislation by President Bill Clinton." There are now more than sixty such corridors throughout the country. "We are still amazingly rural between Boston and Washington, DC. We're still 84 percent open space up here," says Kefalas, noting that it's the last stretch of dark night sky in this section of the East Coast. "You can see the Milky Way here on a nice clear night. We have over five hundred miles of trails for people to mountain bike, hike, and run on." Killingly's top spots sure do rely on Mother Nature. Find outdoor recreation at **Killingly Pond State Park** (**portal.ct.gov/DEEP/ State-Parks/Locate-Park-Forest/Other-State-Parks-and-Forests #KillinglyPond**), 162 acres of hiking, fishing, and boating. **Quinebaug Lake State Park** (**portal.ct.gov/DEEP/State-Parks/Locate-Park-Forest/ Other-State-Parks-and-Forests#QuinebaugLake**) offers a similar experience on 181 acres. This area also includes the **Quinebaug River Trail** (**www.traillink.com/trail/quinebaug-river-trail/**), a

4.8-mile paved pathway, ideal for biking, walking, or jogging. **Old Furnace State Park** is an interesting place, named for an iron furnace that operated there during Revolutionary War times, when iron was used for horseshoes. Many industries were located on this fall line off the Quinebaug River, ripe with rapids

Visit Killingly, part of the Last Green Valley National Heritage Corridor.

Take an adventurous leap with the experts at Skydive Danielson. Jeremy Allen

and waterfalls, where energy was harnessed from the water to power gristmills and sawmills. "It's a great trail walk, it's dog friendly, and any wet areas sport little footbridges," says Jill St. Clair of the Eastern Regional Tourism District, noting a gorgeous spot where hikers can stand and see all the way to Rhode Island. And for you thrill seekers out there, visit **Skydive Danielson (www.skydivedanielson.com)**. Danielson is a borough of Killingly. Even novices can take a tandem skydive, hooked up to a certified instructor. "You have to be relatively physically adept. We do the picnic table test. If you can climb up onto a picnic table and jump off it without hurting yourself or needing assistance, that's a pretty good idea of the amount of physical ability you need to have," says Andy Marcoux, drop zone manager, as well as safety and training advisor. That said, plenty of people qualify. The business even sees many older folks. "We take senior citizens all the time, and they usually say, 'Man, I should have done this earlier,'" says Marcoux, noting that employees are very good at helping participants work through their nerves. "That first two to three seconds after leaving the airplane, your brain goes into overload. You've just done something that evolution has 100 percent told us not to do. Then, once you get over that moment, you're free in the sky. There's everything around you and nothing around you at the same time. It's indescribable, and everyone who lands says, 'I wish I had words to describe what I just felt.'" The business completes about twenty-five hundred tandem skydives per season. "It's nice being up in the Quiet Corner of Connecticut, because it's just a unique area; it is really pretty from altitude, especially in the springtime," says Marcoux, adding that summer and fall are special too. "You can see all the way to Block Island and out to Providence, so it's really gorgeous." Some people with disabilities qualify for jumping. Marcoux has been touched by stories of participants who are blind or have Parkinson's disease, ALS (amyotrophic lateral sclerosis), or Down syndrome. The company has even worked with hospice patients. Skydive Danielson operates from mid-April until October.

Vernon: This rural town is filled with farmland, green and lush this time of year. Vernon is home to the Tankerhoosen River Valley, one of the state's designated greenways. The rail trail is part of the Hop River State Park Trail and runs from Manchester to Willimantic, through Vernon. The valley also includes the Shenipsit Blue Blazed Trail, Valley Falls Park, and the Talcott Ravine Loop. "We have almost forty miles of trails in Vernon, and you can walk from one end of the Tankerhoosen Valley to the other, about 5.5 miles without leaving greenways," says Jon Roe, longtime resident and creator of the **Tankerhoosen (www.tankerhoosen.info)**, which provides comprehensive information about the area. I am a child of the '80s, so guess what? I grew-up spending weekends at the roller rink! That's why I'm partial to sharing information about **Ron-A-Roll Indoor Roller Skating Center (www.ronaroll.com)**, a throwback destination that offers fun for the whole family. This vibrant town also boasts the **New England Civil War Museum (www.newenglandcivilwar museum.com)**, open every Saturday and Sunday with free admission. The museum is accessible for those of all abilities. See artifacts, books, and periodicals. For a different museum experience, check out the **New England Motorcycle Museum (www.newenglandmotorcycle museum.org)**, containing a collection of over one hundred vintage motorcycles and memorabilia housed in a 150,000-square-foot historic textile mill. This wheelchair-accessible museum is open Friday, Saturday, and Sunday. Looking for a dose of agricultural fun? Head to **Strong Family Farm (www.strongfamilyfarm.org)**, which offers gardening and beekeeping classes for the public, along with special programming on Sundays, starting in June. That's when the farm store opens, featuring Connecticut-grown and -produced items. "It's an escape for the

Strong Family Farm, known for its "big yellow barn," is a beloved spot in Vernon. Dan Villeneuve Photography

community. A lot of my friends come back and say it's the only thing they recognize in town because it hasn't changed. It's like a little oasis in the middle of the town; we preserve the whole farm, including the pasture lands," says Nancy Strong, a descendant of the family that built the working farm in 1878. She's also founder of a nonprofit that both saved the farm and established it as an educational center. "People love coming to the farm and going back in time and also enjoying the present, learning about gardening, beekeeping, and all sorts of programs," she says, noting that a springtime Chicken Run 5K is a popular event that supports the farm's endeavors. It's affectionately known to area folks as "the big yellow barn," and folks in wheelchairs navigate the farm relatively well.

Woodbridge: This lovely town is known for its history and land. Check out a unique, fully restored one-room schoolhouse, built in the 1870s. The **Old South School (www.woodbridgehistory.org/old-south-school/)** gives visitors a glimpse at an old-fashioned classroom, complete with antique photos and classic desks. "You get a full immersion experience of what a schoolhouse would have been like more than one hundred years ago," says Alexia Belperron, president of the board of directors of the Amity & Woodbridge Historical Society, which gives tours by request. Anyone can walk around outside. The society can provide a ramp to help those in wheelchairs get inside. The society is headquartered at the **Darling House Museum (www.woodbridgehistory.org/the-darling -house)**, a colonial cape dating back to the 1770s, once home to a prominent local family. "The museum has been described by experts from the state's preservation office as one of the best historic house museums in the state. It really is a remarkable site," says Belperron, emphasizing that much of the house and its contents are frozen in time. "You see the house and the outbuildings in their original settings. You have the house furnished largely with Darling-family pieces, which is unheard of for most museums. It's one of the best-kept secrets in Connecticut." Thomas Darling was a businessman and tutor, credited with bringing the first printing press to the Elm City area. He also knew Benjamin Franklin. "There is a lightning rod on the house in the style created by Benjamin Franklin. So the conjecture is that Darling got that design from him," says Belperron. The house is open by appointment. It's free to visit, but donations are accepted. There's great open space and walking trails behind the house that lead to West Rock Ridge State Park in New Haven. "You can see old stone walls that would have been part of the Darling Farm," says Belperron. Due to its historic nature, the Darling House is not wheelchair accessible. Belperron says the society has plans to provide virtual tours of the home. Like the Darling house, the **Woodbridge Town Green** is on the National Register of Historic Places;

The Darling House is known as one of the best-preserved historic homes in the state.

it is surrounded by buildings of various ages. Woodbridge sports another national landmark, the **Cement Kiln (www.woodbridgehistory.org/ cement-kiln)**, dating back to 1874, an example of nineteenth-century industry.

Greenwich: This affluent shoreline town is known as the Beverly Hills of the East Coast. Expensive shops and gargantuan mansions aside, Greenwich is also rich with culture. The **Bruce Museum (www.brucemuseum.org)** is a one-of-a-kind spot that displays art and more. "The museum has been in operation for more than one hundred years. The first exhibition, in 1912, featured works from members of the Cos Cob Art Colony, made up of Impressionist painters," says Chief Operating Officer Suzanne Lio, explaining

The Bruce Museum in Greenwich recently underwent a sixty-seven-million-dollar expansion. Ben Crowther

that textile merchant Robert Moffat Bruce deeded the building to the town in 1908 to be used as a museum of art, science, and natural history. "We celebrate that by looking at the intersections of art and science and celebrating the collections we've amassed for more than a century." The museum recently underwent a sixty-seven-million-dollar expansion, which tripled its exhibition space. "We really look at the commonalities between art and science. Look at someone like Leonardo Da Vinci. He really had this amazing connection; he was able to look at things with a critical eye that could look at both disciplines, which aren't disparate, if you think about it," says Lio. "We represent a new way of looking at things. We really center on community, art, science, and education. Those are the pillars of our institution, and being able to look at those intersections between art and science really does make us a one-of-a-kind location in the state." The museum is fully accessible to those with physical disabilities, and visitors may borrow a wheelchair if necessary. For outdoor recreation, head to the impressive **Greenwich Audubon Center (www.greenwich.audubon.org)**, with almost three hundred acres and seven miles of walking trails, open seven days a week, dawn to dusk. The grounds include several accessible trails. The center includes a kids' learning center with hands-on activities and natural history exhibits.

For those with mobility issues, the center has an elevator, as well as a wheelchair and scooter that can be borrowed inside the building. In the warm months, the public can take a ferry out to **Great Captain's Island** (**www.greenwichct.gov**), a hot spot for birds such as egrets and herons. Enjoy opportunities for swimming and picnicking.

New Canaan: Head to this beautiful town for a look at the incredibly unique **Glass House** (**www.theglasshouse.org**). "It's a mid-century modern residence designed by architect Philip Johnson in 1949. He lived here on weekends for over fifty years; then it became a museum with the National Trust for Historic Preservation and a historic site," says Communications Director Christa Carr. Tours are available Thursday through Monday, April through December. Tickets must be purchased online in advance. The site is wheelchair accessible. The property includes forty-nine beautiful acres, fourteen structures, and an art collection. Prepare to be inspired on an environmental level. "We are pesticide-free, so we are part of the **Pollinator**

In New Canaan, see the incredibly unique Glass House, designed by architect Philip Johnson. Michael Biondo

Pathway (**www.pollinator-pathway.org/towns-1/connecticut**)," says Carr, referencing a nonprofit, born in Wilton, Connecticut, in 2017, that encourages towns to join to become a network, working together to promote a pollinator-friendly habitat for our wildlife. The Glass House has visitors from all around the world. "It's quite iconic," says Carr. From culture to nature, get your exercise at the **New Canaan Nature Center** (**www.newcanaannature.org**), featuring two miles of trails through both meadows and woodlands. Peruse gardens and a greenhouse or walk through cattails, thanks to a 350-foot boardwalk. This location, open year-round and free of charge, is pet-friendly and ADA compliant.

Stamford: The second-largest city in the state, Stamford is home to a bustling downtown full of great restaurants and shops, along with miles of gorgeous shoreline and some neighborhoods that feel like they're in the burbs. It's also full of culture. Let's begin at the **Stamford Museum & Nature Center** (**www.stamfordmuseum.org**). Folks can enjoy programs such as drive-in movies, farm-to-table suppers, cooking classes, farmer & artisan markets, clambakes, and festivals at this expansive and versatile

Enjoy hiking trails, Heckscher Farm, and fine art at the Stamford Museum & Nature Center. Stamford Museum & Nature Center

location. "With over eighty acres of hardwood forest, miles of hiking trails, and the sixteen-acre heart of our site, the beloved Heckscher Farm, we are the model nature-based organization for getting families outdoors year-round. We revel in intergenerational engagement, offering a rich canvas of programs and events for families, adults, and children alike. We're known for unique social experiences, cultural enrichment, and we love connecting with the natural world around us in simple, elegant ways," says Chief Executive Officer Melissa H. Mulrooney, adding that in addition to this natural world, people can find incredible art at this location. "When visitors walk into the Stamford Museum, they invariably know it was once someone's private residence, and they are often surprised to learn that it was in fact the brainchild and heart's desire of department store magnate and mogul Henri Bendel. We host or curate six major fine-art exhibitions in our Bendel Mansion Museum Galleries annually and have grown a diverse permanent collection of more than twenty thousand cultural objects, artifacts, and works of art since our founding in 1936." The museum and farmhouse are both accessible for those with mobility issues. Visitors can navigate Heckscher Farm on smooth looping paths that are wheelchair friendly. Additionally, Wheels on Woods is a universally accessible trail, giving folks of all abilities the opportunity to enjoy nature. This destination also includes a planetarium, open for special groups and events. For more outdoor activity, check out **Goodbody Garden & Fort Stamford (www.good bodygarden.wordpress.com**), a place to reflect and learn about Revolutionary War history. Visitors can still see mounds of earth that were part of a fort, protecting local soldiers from the British back in the late 1700s.

Rocky Hill: Take a turn off Interstate 91 to find a gem of a spot. **Dinosaur State Park (www.dinosaurstatepark.org)**, open since 1968, shows off one of the largest dinosaur track sites in North America underneath a supercool geodesic dome. "We have more than 750 Jurassic-era footprints on display," says Environmental Education Coordinator Mike Ross. "They were discovered by accident in 1966 when they were building the basement foundation for a state laboratory." Folks can stroll through a comprehensive display of early Jurassic tracks made by behemoths like *Dilophosaurus*, which roamed our state two hundred million years ago, during the dawn of the dinosaurs. The tracks are so well preserved because a valley was created during the breakup of Pangaea. Sediment from the mountains was washed into this area, as well as ocean water. "In Connecticut we have sedimentary rock, which

Stroll through an incredible display of early Jurassic tracks at Dinosaur State Park in Rocky Hill.

is where fossils are found. It is very special; a lot of Connecticut is metamorphic rock, but the center of Connecticut is that sedimentary rock," says Ross, noting that a lake was formed at this site in prehistoric times. "It was a location that dinosaurs really wanted to come to for fishing purposes and social matters." The track area was designated a National Natural Landmark by the US Department of Interior in order to preserve it for generations to come. "We have a lot of interactive exhibits inside the center that promote working together as a family. We really encourage parents and kids to do these activities together because we're all lifelong learners," says Ross. In addition to the indoor fun, find two miles of easy-to-navigate nature trails, including swamps and meadows, and the Dinosaur State Park Arboretum. "There are over 250 Jurassic-era species of plants here. We have magnolias and evergreens," says Ross. Visitors can make their own plaster cast of a real dinosaur track and also take part in gem and fossil mining. The exhibit center is wheelchair accessible. Nearby is the **Rocky Hill-Glastonbury Ferry** (**portal.ct.gov/ DOT/Traveler/ferries/Rocky-Hill-Ferry**), the oldest continuously operating ferry service in the country; it runs between April and November. The flat, open *Hollister III* is both fun and useful.

Wethersfield: This special place, founded in 1633 and known as "Ye Most Ancient Towne," is filled with beautiful colonial homes. The **Webb Deane Stevens Museum** (**www.wdsmuseum.org**) is located in the heart of the oldest historic district in the state. This cultural spot, open weekends in April and regular hours May through October, is composed of three homes that span three centuries. The first is the Joseph Webb House, built in 1752. "That is the house where George Washington met with French general Rochambeau; they planned what eventually became the Battle of Yorktown, which ended the American Revolution," says Cynthia Joseph Riccio, associate director and director of visitor engagement, noting that the second house was built in the 1760s and belonged to Silas Deane. "We loosely call Silas Deane the first diplomat, because he was instrumental in securing a lot of the help from the French that helped us win the American Revolution. Then we have the Isaac Stevens house, built between 1788 and 1789; that's really the house where we show how time went from the colonial era into the early to mid-1800s." The grounds also include an education center, a historic barn, and a Colonial Revival garden. The first floor of the Webb house, the museum shop, the education center, and exhibit galleries are wheelchair accessible. The Deane and Stevens houses are not, due to the age of the buildings. Charming downtown Wethersfield is filled with unique restaurants and shops. "The stakeholders and businesses in and around Main Street all work very well together to bring people here and keep people here. You can get something to eat, you can visit a museum, you can shop, you can get ice cream, you can walk around," says Riccio, also pointing to the **Wethersfield Historical Society** (**www.wethersfieldhistory.org**), which offers tours of the **Hurlbut-Dunham House**, free of charge from May through October. Even though this historic home, dating back to the 1790s, was originally owned by a mariner who traveled the globe, it also has a fascinating history of strong women who kept the house and its history going. The society is raising money to add a wheelchair ramp to the house. Each year, the society also offers unique walking tours about the architecture and history of the old homes and houses of worship. "People like to be outdoors these days. It's one of the good things that came out of COVID, an appreciation of the outdoors," says Dorene Coarcia, a volunteer and board president of the society. Also see history from the water thanks to **Slipaway River Tours** (**www .slipawayrivertours.com**), which works out of three locations, including Wethersfield Cove. "The cove has a ton of history; it was one of the earliest settlements," says owner Bill Keyt, who shows groups of up to sixteen people a water view of antique buildings. "It's been enjoyable to introduce people to this gem of ours, the Connecticut River." He's been providing narrated tours for visitors, including information about geography, history, and nature, for the past few years. In addition to the learning, folks can listen to music, relax, and soak up the gorgeous scenery. "You go around a bend and you're looking at vistas that the early settlers or even the Algonquins would have seen, because the shoreline looks almost no different in various spots," says Keyt.

Beautiful Old Wethersfield Center contains the Webb Deane Stevens Museum and the Hurlbut-Dunham House.

Bloomfield: When the flowers begin to bloom, head to **Auerfarm** (**www.auerfarm.org**), a natural destination committed to getting families outdoors, named for the Auerbach family that owned the famed department store G. Fox & Co. "The 4-H education Auerfarm is a 120-acre farm. We are open to the public 365 days a year. There's no charge for the public to come and visit," says Executive Director Erica Fearn, noting that this location is all about hands-on education. "You can come out and

Kids can roam, explore, and connect with nature at Auerfarm in Bloomfield. Low Tide Photography

visit the animals. We have cows, chickens, ducks, geese, alpacas, peacocks, sheep, goats, and mini horses." Rent a small plot in a community garden or stroll past the Master Gardener's garden, managed by the **UConn Master Gardener program (www.mastergardener.uconn.edu)**, which donates all of its produce to FoodShare to help feed the hungry. "Then we have the lovely nourishing garden, which is a place you can go and sit, feel the sun and the breeze on your face, listen to the birds. It's just a place where you can enjoy the flowers and herbs," says Fearn. More than forty kids involved in 4-H visit the farm twice a month. But all kids can roam, explore, and connect with nature. "It's a great place to reset, a great place to put your hands in the dirt and let kids run around and be free," says Fearn. "We have a play forest, which is the perfect place for children to touch things. They can touch wood chips, move rocks around. They can make a fort or build a fairy house." Some areas are accessible for those with mobility issues. The Auerbach family also donated a forty-acre parcel of land to the state, now the **Auerfarm State Park Scenic Reserve (portal.ct.gov/DEEP/State-Parks/Parks/Auerfarm-State-Park)**, an ideal spot for hiking and birding. Also be sure to explore **Penwood State Park (portal.ct.gov/DEEP/State-Parks/Parks/Penwood-State-Park)**, with eight hundred acres, great for hiking buffs.

UNIQUE OUTINGS FOR SPRING

What says "New England" more than an old red barn, set in a field of wildflowers? Nothing. That's why you should check out a state-sponsored effort that's all about the history and preservation of an iconic structure. The **Connecticut Barn Trail** (***www.cttrust.org*** and ***www.connecticutbarns.org***) was born circa 2010, after volunteers took action to save these charming buildings. Sites include Bristol's Farm in Canton, open to the public. Along the trail in North Granby, is a quiet spot called Lost Acres Orchard, home to two classic barns that lean up against each other, supported by old-fashioned planks and pegs. Also see Cold Spring Farm in Avon and Perry's Farm in Collinsville. The Hill-Stead Museum in Farmington also sports several rustic structures. The Hay Barn, built in 1898 and located along US 4, features a classic gambrel roof and was used to shelter the dairy herd. While the Hay Barn and an adjoining structure are not open to the public, they certainly add to the property's character. The Carriage Barn at the Hill-Stead Museum represents a "connected house and barn." It's now used to host weddings and receptions. (Learn more about the Hill-Stead Museum in the "Winter" section of this book.)

Take yourself on a driving tour of the Connecticut Barn Trail to see these New England buildings, full of history.

Every spring in April, Thomas the Tank Engine makes a stop at the **Essex Steam Train & Riverboat**. As a resident of this beautiful town, and as a mom to two boys who once adored this affable blue train, I love to see him chug by with smiling little faces peeking out the windows. This destination also hosts a regular dinner train that's become popular over the years, offering visitors a good meal and incredible vistas of a beautiful area while enjoying the ambience of a historic locomotive. Additionally, visitors can get a wonderful one-two punch with a train ride to Deep River Landing to board the Becky Thatcher, the company's riverboat, which gives folks a relaxing ride with views of the Connecticut River.

There's never a dull moment aboard the Becky Thatcher, operated by Essex Steam Train & Riverboat. Tom Nanos Photography

Speaking of the **Essex Steam Train & Riverboat**, during the pandemic this iconic business diversified to add an activity that's become very popular: rail biking (***www.essexsteamtrain. com/experiences/rail-bike-2/***). "We were seeing many people trying it because it was

something different. It was something new," says Bob Wuchert, vice president of the Essex Steam Train & Riverboat, noting that this activity got people outside in the heart of the COVID era. Imagine a contraption that is part bike, part locomotive, and entirely powered by your feet. Choose a bike with either two or four seats. Folks literally ride the rails at a speed of about eight miles per hour, past vistas that are both busy and serene. After doing several stories about this activity, I brought my family along for a ride! We operated a four-seater together, and, believe it or not, it was a hit, even with the teens, who are notoriously difficult to please! Now that the train is back to running at full capacity, rail bike adventures are pop-up events, offering seven- to ten-mile excursions,

Take friends or family on a unique and fun trip along the tracks during a rail bike tour, courtesy of Essex Steam Train & Riverboat. Tom Nanos Photography

round-trip. Several different route options are offered. Head from Essex to Old Saybrook or from Essex to Deep River. The season runs from June through October.

What kid isn't mesmerized by dinosaurs? The state tourism department came up with a cute idea to engage families: the **Connecticut Dinosaur Trail** (*www.ctvisit.com/listings/ connecticut-dinosaur-trail*). See an animatronic Dilophosaurus at the Connecticut Science Center, or see real-life skeletons at the Yale Peabody Museum of Natural History. See actual Jurassic-era footprints at Dinosaur State Park and stroll past more than sixty life-size dinosaurs on a wooded trail at the Dinosaur Place at Nature's Art Village.

The kids will love to traverse the state's Dinosaur Trail, with stops in New Haven and Rocky Hill!

Need a perfect spot for a family photo? Look no further. As spring turns into summer, head to a Hartford spot that's well-known for its beauty. **Elizabeth Park** (***www.elizabethparkct.org***) is the perfect place to tiptoe through the tulips in April, thanks to the colorful Robert A. Prill Tulip Garden. Then, by late June, the Helen S. Kaman Rose Garden is in full bloom. The park is filled with 476 varieties of the romantic flower, draping over arches and within views of historic buildings. The park, on the site of a former working farm, is open every day from sunrise to sunset. The public can visit this 102-acre park, on the National Register of Historic Places, free of charge. The Rose Garden is fully accessible.

Nothing beats an early summer trip to Elizabeth Park in Hartford for a walk around the sumptuous Rose Garden.

Also see gorgeous flowers at **Wicked Tulips** (***www.wickedtulips.com***) in Preston. Go online to buy a token—much cheaper than paying in-person—which gets you a stroll around this incredible farm to pick ten luscious blooms. Picking more flowers will cost you additional money. But I'm here to tell you that it's worth it. What a magical place! Experience a huge field full of tulips of all glorious colors. A walk through the aisles is so peaceful. Look around and see families taking selfies, kids sitting on play tractors, and folks simply enjoying themselves in the sun. The farm is wheelchair accessible. Don't miss a visit here!

Prepare for an incredible experience when you visit Wicked Tulips in Preston in the springtime.

Take a boat tour and enjoy a restaurant like Abbott's Lobster in the Rough during a wonderful Connecticut summer.

Summer

What can I say, I'm a summer girl. And I'm so lucky to live in a spot where I can enjoy the season's gifts to the fullest. Gaze upon a lighthouse while embarking on one of the many cruises that show off our gorgeous coastline. Pick a strawberry at a local farm and taste the sweetness. Stroll around an animal haven during the kids' break from school. And don't forget to indulge in that ice cream, smothered in sprinkles! Here are ways to savor the season in all sections of the state.

Killingworth: There's a spot in this rural town that literally turns purple sometime from late June through August, usually peaking in July. **Lavender Pond Farm (www.lavenderpondfarm.com)** is a breezy spot with a fascinating history. In 2014, Denise Salafia purchased the property with a mission to make it something special. She had read a book titled *Miss Rumphius* with her ailing mother. The book is about adding beauty to the world around us. So when Salafia's mom passed away, she knew how to fulfill her mission by also honoring her memories. "She turned all the fields into lavender fields, and over the years we've grown little by little to make the world a more beautiful place," says niece Savannah Falcone, who works in the office at the farm. Folks can walk through a labyrinth, past a gazebo and chicken coop to gaze at honeybee hives, and take in the beauty of the farm. "You can wander behind the barn. We have our Fairy Stroll, which is around the pond. In the woods, you can see fairy gardens. Walk around and see how many you can find," says Falcone. Explore the lovely gift shop and take a ride on a small electric train that kids love, winding visitors through the incredible grounds during peak season. "It's definitely a moment of peace. We want you to enjoy being here, enjoy the serenity of it all, and just leave happy. That's our goal," says Falcone. The farm is fully accessible. Right around the corner is **Parmelee Farm (www .parmeleefarm.org)**, purchased by the town in 2000. On the State Register of Historic Places, this gorgeous 132-acre farm sports hiking trails, little free libraries, a community garden, summer concerts, and a

Left: Find beauty and serenity at Lavender Pond Farm, especially when the purple flower is in bloom.
Right: Historic Parmelee Farm offers summer concerts and great hiking trails.

striking red farmhouse, open frequently for tours. Parking for those of all abilities is available.

New London: New London is a cool city with a historical vibe, full of nautical charm. It's home to a transportation center where passengers can board ferries to Long Island, New York and Block Island, Rhode Island. There's also a ferry to Fishers Island but be warned: this elusive and exclusive community is very private and not particularly interested in tourists. But, when it's not engaged in trips to Long Island, **Cross Sound Ferry** (**www.longislandferry.com**) takes passengers on a high-speed lighthouse cruise that's a really enjoyable outing. In speedy, agile style, the large boat zips around to eight lighthouses, including North Dumpling Light, on an island owned by Segway scooter inventor Dean Kamen. The quirky island also sports a duck boat and a small replica of Stonehenge. Speaking of lighthouses, my favorite Connecticut beacon just happens to be **New London Ledge Light** (**www.sites.google.com/ view/ledge-light-foundation/home**), which looks like a large red home, looming out of the center of the Thames River. Every summer, the **New London Custom House Maritime Museum** (**www.nlmaritime society.org**) shuttles folks by boat to this incredible beacon, site of an infamous ghost story about a keeper named Ernie. And that's not all. The society also takes folks out to two other lighthouses, **Little Gull** and **Race Rock**, particularly difficult to get to safely due to the strong currents that surround it. The maritime society also brings visitors into the **New London Harbor Lighthouse**, one of the oldest lighthouses in the country. The stately white cylinder can be approached by land and features a 116-step climb to the lantern room. The museum itself

Ferries from New London's transportation center take visitors to Long Island and Block Island.

houses an incredible collection of unique artifacts, such as vintage diving helmets, ship models, and a Fresnel lens. "Everything we have is local and authentic," says Susan Tamulevich, the museum's executive director. The museum's lower level is accessible for those of all abilities; feel free to contact them to inquire about further accommodations. The museum also houses the esteemed *Amistad* exhibit, a comprehensive look at the famous slave ship that was overtaken by captives on a journey from Cuba. The **Hempsted Houses (www.ctlandmarks.org/properties/hempsted-houses/**) also examine the state's complicated relationship with slavery. The museum, which is not wheelchair accessible, tells the story of Adam Jackson, enslaved by Joshua Hempsted, a farmer and judge in the 1700s. These impactful stories and many more are told on the city's **Black Heritage Trail (www.visitnewlondon.org/black-heritage-trail/**), a fascinating celebration of strength and resilience. There's Revolutionary War history in this maritime mecca, as well. At **Fort Trumbull State Park (portal.ct.gov/DEEP/State-Parks/Parks/Fort-Trumbull-State-Park**), folks can learn history and walk around the massive fort with incredible views of the Thames River. Also find a boardwalk and a fishing pier. The original fort was built in 1777 to protect the harbor from a British invasion. But infamous traitor Benedict Arnold led troops to storm this area and took control of both Fort Trumbull and Fort Griswold (see our section on the city of Groton). The fort that stands today was constructed in the 1840s to hold large artillery pieces. Over the years, it has housed research facilities and training schools. Twentieth-century scientists even developed sonar, undersea war technology, in this location that was integral to American strategy during World War II. Visitors can tour the fort and see where soldiers slept at night and ate their meals. The visitor center has videos, interactive exhibits, and dioramas. Folks can build a virtual fort. The park is accessible for all visitors and features an on-site elevator. New London Harbor is home port to the **Coast Guard's Tall Ship,** *Eagle,* often on display during the annual **Sail Fest (www.sailfest .org),** held every July. For a peaceful experience, visit the **Lyman Allyn Art Museum (www.lymanallyn.org),** with a collection of more than

eighteen thousand paintings, sculptures, drawings, and other art forms. See works from well-known artists such as Andrew Wyeth, Winslow Homer, and Sol LeWitt. The accessible museum can loan visitors a wheelchair if necessary. Oh my goodness, we had so many fun days at **Ocean Beach Park (www .ocean-beach-park.com),** called "New England's finest sugar sand beach and boardwalk attraction." A visit here feels like a throwback to simpler times. The beach is fantastic, perfect for a fun swim with the kids. But the park also features water slides, amusement rides, and even an Olympic-size pool. Finish a hot day with a cool ice cream. There's nothing

See incredible lighthouses, such as the New London Harbor Lighthouse, during tours around New London.

better. The boardwalk is wheelchair accessible, with ramps leading to the beach. Regarding access on the sand, General Manager Dave Sugrue invites folks to give him a call. He will arrange for a gator or golf cart to help anyone with a mobility issue down to the water. Connect with nature at the **Connecticut College Arboretum (www.conncoll.edu/ the-arboretum/),** 750 beautiful acres filled with a plant collection and natural areas. Docent-led tours are offered spring through fall. This location is not accessible for wheelchairs. Lastly, take a one-hour guided tour of the **Shaw Mansion (www.nlchs.org/about/shaw-mansion),** the state's naval war office during the American Revolution. The first floor of the mansion is wheelchair accessible.

Groton: This coastal city, known as the "Submarine Capital of the World," is home to the Electric Boat Division of General Dynamics, maker of subs since World War II, along with the Naval Submarine Base New London.

"Groton is rich in history. It doesn't belong to you; it doesn't belong to me. It belongs to everyone, and we have to share it," says Jim Streeter, former mayor and historian. "The submarine base and the personnel are an integral part of Groton." While visitors can occasionally see these incredible warships surface and cruise along the water's edge, folks can always experience one at the **Submarine Force Museum** (**www.ussnautilus.org**), a favorite destination for me and my sons. Head into the twenty-seven-thousand-square-foot museum to see a rare collection of more than thirty-thousand submarine-related artifacts. "With Groton

Take the kids through small spaces to experience life on the USS Nautilus *at the Submarine Force Museum.*

being the home of the submarine force, it's a nice, natural draw," says Admiral John Padgett (ret.), president of the Submarine Force Library and Museum Association, an independent group that raises money to support this destination. "The museum provides some things you can touch. They have an interactive program." The biggest relic is the USS *Nautilus*, the first nuclear-powered submarine in the world, launched in 1955 and decommissioned in 1980, after traveling to the North Pole during the Cold War. It's really amazing to climb through the small doors and explore this incredible underwater ship, seeing how its residents ate in the mess hall and slept in cramped bunks. But it's important to know that touring the submarine means enduring tight spaces. Unlike the museum, it is not accessible for those in wheelchairs. Find scavenger hunts, self-guided tours, a museum theater, and an augmented reality experience in the museum, which also houses a library with thousands

Project Oceanology operates out of UConn's Avery Point campus.

of nautical documents and photos. Admission to this museum, closed on Tuesdays, is free. This coastal area was also home to one of the nation's largest nineteenth-century whaling ports, as well as infamous battles during the Revolutionary War. A visit to **Fort Griswold Battlefield State Park (portal.ct.gov/DEEP/State-Parks/Parks/Fort-Griswold-Battlefield -State-Park)** is meaningful, giving folks a chance to learn and reflect. On this site in 1781, British forces led by Benedict Arnold overtook a fort, killing eighty-eight American soldiers. Visitors see the remains of a fort, along with a 135-foot monument. There's a museum on-site, as well as the restored **Ebenezer Avery House**, where the wounded recovered after the bloody battle. The park and museum are accessible for all visitors. Colonel William Ledyard lost his life in the battle, killed with his own sword by a British soldier. He is buried nearby in a historic spot aptly called **Colonel Ledyard Cemetery**. On weekends in summer, take advantage of the unique **Thames River Heritage Park Water Taxi (www.thamesriverheritagepark.org/water-taxi/)**, running between Groton and New London, with stops at the city pier, Fort Griswold, and Fort Trumbull. It offers a one-hour, hop-on/hop-off cruise aboard a US Navy "liberty" utility boat, once used to shuttle sailors to shore from big ships. One year, I asked to spend my birthday at **Bluff Point State Park (portal.ct.gov/DEEP/State-Parks/Parks/Bluff-Point-State-Park)**. This coastal reserve is an exceedingly gorgeous spot with sweeping, sparkling views of Long Island Sound. It is the last large parcel of undeveloped land on the Connecticut coastline. Native Americans from the Pequot tribe fished here before it became the site of a plantation in the late 1600s. In the early 1900s, Bluff Point was home to summer cottages and a seasonal camping community. The famous hurricane of 1938, one of the deadliest and most destructive storms ever to hit New England, decimated these homes. The 3.6-mile loop is flat and easy terrain for able walkers of any age or ability. The park requires all dogs to be leashed. Some areas of the park are wheelchair accessible. Now that the boys are older, we partake in an activity that's both educational and thrilling. **Mystic Boat Adventures (www.mysticboatadventures.com)** in the village of Noank invites folks to tour the coast while operating a two-person pontoon boat called a Craig Cat. Business owner Rob Roache leads the pack, giving facts about landmarks such as the Mystic Seaport Museum and the iconic Bascule Bridge (see the "Mystic" section for more information). The outing turns exciting when he invites drivers to find some speed, do some doughnuts,

Left: Participants see the Mystic Seaport Museum and Latimer Reef Lighthouse during a super-fun Mystic Boat Adventure. Right: Take the kids and leashed pups on a walk around incredibly gorgeous Bluff Point State Park, with rocks for climbing and views for savoring.

and experience what these agile boats can do! As a grand finale, visitors speed out to **Latimer Reef Light**, located in an area that encompasses New York, Connecticut, and Rhode Island. Also get a view of the **Morgan Point Lighthouse**, originally built in 1831 then expanded into a fabulous privately owned home. **Project Oceanology (www.oceanology.org)**, a nonprofit education and research group located on **UConn's Avery Point campus (www.averypoint.uconn.edu)**, offers unique public cruises. Throughout the summer, take a trip out onto the water on the *Enviro-Lab* research vessel. Guides throw a net into the water to scoop up sea life, which is then studied by guests and then returned to the water. Project Oceanology works with families to make the boat as accessible as possible.

Mystic: Mystic is actually a village in the towns of Groton and Stonington, but I'm bending the rules and giving it a section. I have to! Mystic is incredible, a perfect day trip destination. There's so much to talk about, so let's begin at the **Mystic Seaport Museum** (**www.mysticseaport.org**), which offers a unique stroll

Downtown Mystic is home to the iconic bascule bridge.

through a re-created seaside village from the nineteenth century. See an old-fashioned school, bank, doctor's office, and pharmacy. My boys used to love the on-site Children's Museum, where kids can play on pretend boats. There's also a planetarium and a gallery with rotating exhibits. But it's the old ships, available for touring, that really make an impact. Climb aboard the **Charles W. Morgan whaleship** or the **L. A. Dunton fishing schooner** to see how whalers and fishermen lived, for months at a time, out on the open ocean. The *Sabino*, a National Historic Landmark, is a steamboat built in 1908 to ferry passengers and cargo between towns in Maine. It's currently the oldest coal-fired vessel in operation. It hit the water again during the summer 2023 after a pandemic break. Visitors can see the fascinating engine room and employees shoveling coal during a cruise. The seaport prides itself on giving folks opportunities to get out on the water. "The Seaport is such a dynamic place, there's really something for everyone," says Sophia Matsas, director of marketing and communications. "Anybody that enjoys getting out on the water can do it in a variety of ways, from renting a pedal boat, a sailboat, or a rowboat. They can take cruises along the river." Recently, the *Mystic Seaport Express* was launched, offering service from downtown. The fare includes a half-hour ride and admission to the museum. Every summer the museum hosts events such as River Fest, with live music and the Wooden Boat Show. The museum has ADA-compliant walkways and has plans to add tactile experiences and audio tours for blind or print-challenged visitors. The museum also aims to provide access below the deck of the *L. A. Dunton* with an ADA-compliant lift. The postcard-worthy downtown area sports excellent restaurants and lovely shops. In this area, you can also hop on board the **Argia** (**www.argiamystic.com**). This modern replica of a nineteenth-century sailing schooner is docked in a convenient spot for tourists to come aboard. At the start of the trip, passengers see the Mystic Seaport Museum from a new perspective. After the museum, the ship heads down the Mystic River and underneath the bascule bridge, another National Historic Landmark. Then the sails are raised as the crew asks the passengers to participate. The eighty-one-foot vessel, modeled after a Chesapeake Bay schooner, holds up to forty-nine passengers who head out to Fishers Island Sound, where the crew shares facts about the exclusive island and surrounding landmasses. Tours aboard the *Argia* run from May through October, and visitors can choose a half-day

Argia is a replica schooner that takes passengers out into Fishers Island Sound.

excursion or a sunset cruise. The *Argia* is not wheelchair accessible but can accommodate those with walkers or canes. Also downtown, sign up for some spooky time with **Seaside Shadows** (**www.seasideshadows .com**), which offers haunted history tours of this classic maritime village. Take the Original Ghost Walk, which lasts two hours and spans about a mile, past the bascule bridge. Hear the facts and folklore of this seaside village. Visitors will be treated to stories involving the Revolutionary and Civil Wars. The Mystic Moonlit Graveyard Ghost Tour takes participants into a colonial cemetery from the 1660s, where the guide tells spooky, historic tales. The two-hour tour is called a blend of history and mystery! Participants for both tours must be age eleven and up. The **Mystic Aquarium** (**www.maritimeaquarium.org**) is a hugely popular New England destination with thousands of species of marine mammals, fish, invertebrates, and reptiles. It was one of my sons' favorite places for a good decade or so. Several times a year, we would while away hours at the aquarium, staring at the colorful fish, searching for the moray eel, and listening to the sounds at the interactive marsh exhibit. Outside the main building is a tank for the gorgeous beluga whales. Juno, a particularly charismatic male whale, is the most famous of the bunch. He's known to greet visitors with a smile and even swim around in tune to music. Down the way, find the African penguins. The animal shows in the theater are delightful. Watch the California sea lions perform tricks in and out of a pool of water. The aquarium also offers exciting encounter programs with belugas, penguins, and seals. You can either have an

The whole family will love a trip to Mystic Aquarium, with its plethora of fish, encounter programs, and visits with the charismatic beluga whales.

"up-close" experience with them or paint with them. There are even encounters with rays, jellyfish, and reptiles, along with the opportunity to be a marine biologist for a day. The aquarium is accessible for all, and on-site wheelchairs can be borrowed. Looking for a simple day out in nature? Head to the **Denison Pequotsepos Nature Center** (**www.dpnc .org**) to explore a natural-history museum with exhibits detailing the state's forests, meadows, and wetlands. Meet a variety of small creatures, such as frogs, fish, and snakes. Head into a cool little movie theater for a show called *Night in the Meadow*. See owls, a falcon, and hawks, all native to the area, in an outdoor enclosure before heading out on the trails that surround the beautiful property. You can even utilize the inventive Borrow a Backpack program, enabling visitors to bring supplies for birding or forest exploration out on the trails. Some trails feature gentle grades and level ground for those with mobility issues. DPNC also offers guided hikes at wheelchair-accessible properties.

See the incredible sites of the Mystic Seaport Museum on land or on the water.

Waterford: Harkness Memorial State Park (portal.ct.gov/DEEP/ State-Parks/Parks/Harkness-Memorial-State-Park) is simply a gem in our state, one I've always loved to visit. Walk around Eolia, the Harkness family's Roman Renaissance Revival mansion, set on a spectacular piece of land that spans more than 230 acres of lawns, gardens, and panoramic views of Long Island Sound. The family summered here in the early 1900s before donating the property to the state in 1950. Folks can fish, picnic, or stroll around the grounds and gardens, but swimming is not allowed at this state park. The mansion is a popular spot for weddings and private parties. Friends of Harkness volunteer docents offer guided tours of the mansion on weekends from Memorial Day through Labor Day. The park and mansion are wheelchair accessible. Families

Stroll the gardens at the incredible Harkness Memorial State Park, a gorgeous gem on the Connecticut coastline.

love to spend an afternoon or evening at the **New London–Waterford Speedbowl (www.speedbowlct.com)**, featuring NASCAR stock car auto racing on an oval track that's three-eighths of a mile long. There is some on-site accessibility for those with mobility issues. For a real treat, head to the **Eugene O'Neill Theater Center (www.theoneill.org)**, named for the four-time Pulitzer Prize winner and the country's only playwright to

See new works of art and performance each summer at the Eugene O'Neill Theater Center in Waterford.

win the Nobel Prize in Literature. The impressive center is really a complex, with housing for actors and several theaters, including outdoor spaces. This spot is known to showcase new voices and new works in the theater world. "I think the O'Neill rises to the top on a national and international scale," says Tony Sheridan, president & CEO of the **Chamber of Commerce of Eastern Connecticut (www.chamberect.com)**, of the work done at the center. He also comments on the stunning location, which he believes inspires creativity. "There's an absolutely gorgeous untouched beach with panoramic views of Long Island Sound. It's probably one of the finest beaches in the state of Connecticut," he says. Each summer kicks off with programming surrounding the art of puppetry. In 2016 then President Barack Obama awarded the center with the National Medal of Arts, celebrating its commitment to culture. Public performances in the ADA-compliant spaces run from June through August. On the beach scene, visit **Waterford Beach Park (www.waterfordct.org/267/Recreation-Parks)** to experience a quarter-mile stretch of sand that shows off an intact dune system in the state. Out-of-towners can buy a day pass to enjoy swimming, fishing, and more. The **Waterford Historical Society (www.waterfordcthistoricalsociety.org)** offers some interesting tours of landmarks around town, such as the 1740 Jordan Schoolhouse, the oldest building in town, as well as the Stacey Barn, with its comprehensive collection of antique farming equipment.

Brooklyn: Each year in August, this beautiful rural town in the state's northeastern Quiet Corner offers an event beloved by thousands. The **Brooklyn Fair** is the oldest continuously active agricultural fair in the country, dating back to 1809. "We've been at it a long time," says president of the fair Ryan Vertefeuille, noting that it's all run by a group of

The Brooklyn Fair is the oldest continuously active agricultural fair in the country. Laura Stone Photography

dedicated volunteers. "It's a good reason to stop working and enjoy some time with the family." Find livestock, fun food, carnival rides, contests, music, and more. Vertefeuille says it's all about providing a tech-free, traditional experience for families while adding some new, unexpected attractions, like PlayLand, each year. "It's an area where parents can sit down and let their children play. There are different kinds of small events and things that kids can do. It doesn't cost the parents anything for them to be there," he explains. "People want to see what they saw at the fair when they were a kid, but they don't want to see the same thing every year. You have to keep them interested." **Creamery Brook Bison Farm (www.creamerybrookbison .net)** opened in 1990, selling meat to consumers. But the farm offers public programs, too, like a festival in June.

Take the kids to Creamery Brook Bison Farm for a lesson on where food comes from.

"Every summer lately, we've been doing a festival here at the farm; we bring in a lot of crafters and music and donkey rides. All day long, we do wagon rides to see the bison," says owner Deb Tanner, who offers private tours all year long to groups of any size. "We want them to see life

99

on a farm. We have a captive audience, so we want to tell them where their food comes from. It doesn't start at a big box store. It starts in the ground or in the barn." There's no other location quite like it in the state. "We're definitely unique," says Tanner. One wagon can accommodate wheelchairs. And folks with mobility issues can navigate somewhat around the farmyard. The **Brooklyn Historical Society Museum** (**www .brooklynct.org/historical-society**) tells the story of the town's well-known Revolutionary War hero, Israel Putnam, a farmer and citizen soldier. It also displays town treasures, such as an antique silk dress and a fork used for ice harvesting. The museum has wheelchair access and an accessible restroom. Nearby, find the **Daniel Putnam Tyler Law Office Museum**, dedicated to Putnam's great-grandson, who served as a county court judge and secretary of state. The museums are located next to a large, beautiful memorial dedicated to Putnam.

Branford: The **Thimble Island Cruise** (**www.thimbleislandcruise .com**) is an institution in this remarkably unique and stunning area thanks to Captain Mike Infantino, who operates the *Sea Mist*. "There are twenty-five inhabited islands; there are approximately ninety-five

The incredibly unique Thimble Islands are an archipelago of small islands, some inhabited, in Long Island Sound.

homes," says this master tour guide, who has been showing off this location, which stands out in all of New England, for the past forty-four years. "There's nothing like it on the coast. Occasionally we see seals. We point out some of the wildlife, like blue herons and great white egrets." This archipelago of small islands on Long Island Sound, visible from the shore of Stony Creek, a section of Branford, are home to everything from mansions to beach cottages. Visitors on the forty-five-minute cruise will see the sites while also hearing tales of pirates and doubloons. "We tell folklore about Captain Kidd the pirate. We bring visitors up to Kidd's island and tell them a little history," says Infantino, noting that the notorious pirate supposedly buried treasure there in the late 1600s. The *Sea Mist*, which sails from May to October, is also available for private charters. The lower deck area of the boat can accommodate wheelchairs. Infantino has recently added a new boat to the fleet. *Island Time* takes folks on pleasure cruises—sans narration—for a different experience in the waters off Branford. Nearby, tour the thirty-thousand-square-foot facility at **Stony Creek Brewery**, home to craft beer and great water views. Folks can bring their own food or buy eats from a food truck before playing bocce or cornhole on the gorgeous grounds. This location is ADA compliant. The beautiful **Legacy Theatre** (**www.legacytheatrect .org**) is also tucked into the little seaside village of Stony Creek. Once a rundown puppet theater, the Legacy has been recently restored and features new amenities in this fresh space, accessible for all. The theater presents musicals, plays, and concerts.

Canaan/Falls Village: Head to the northwestern edge of Connecticut to enjoy an adventure like none other: a **Backyard Adventure UTV Tour** (**www.backyardadventuretours.com**). "It's pretty unique in that we have access to one thousand acres that's all on private property. When you go out on a tour, it's just you, your tour guide, and whoever else is in your group. You get to go out and see nothing but woods and wildlife and a lot of cool scenery," says owner Len Allyn. "Our terrain is pretty complex, so everyone who does a tour basically is glad they're guided; if they weren't, they'd have no idea where to go, because our property is so vast." From a particularly beautiful spot, see all the way into Massachusetts and New York. Four people, max, are allowed in the utility task vehicle. Tours can last sixty or ninety

Experience Connecticut's vistas and landscapes while driving a utility task vehicle. Backyard Adventure UTV Tour

See and hear talented musicians at Music Mountain, the oldest continuing summer chamber music festival in the United States. Anne Day

minutes. Allyn says safety is the company's number-one priority, and participants get some basic training on the UTV. "They operate just like a car. So all we require is that you have a valid driver's license. If you can drive a car confidently, you can navigate a UTV without any problems," he says. "People can take a break from city life and have a lot of fun on a UTV and not spend a fortune." Or experience the hills in a different way—when they are alive with the sounds of Bach, Schubert, Strauss, and Mendelssohn. Falls Village is a village within the town of Canaan, home to a summer music festival much like Tanglewood in the Berkshires. Welcome to **Music Mountain** (**www.musicmountain.org**), the oldest continuing summer chamber music festival in the United States, dating back to 1930. "It's very casual. This was a farm before it became Music Mountain. People love the friendly environment. They come early, they get an ice cream. Sometimes they bring their own picnic," says Artistic and Executive Director Oskar Espina Ruiz. "All of the concerts we present are indoors in Gordon Hall, which is air-conditioned. It holds up to three hundred people. The acoustics are really special for classical music." Folks can stay on the lawn and listen to an audio stream of the concert from the hall. Each summer from June to September, about seventeen chamber music concerts take place on Sundays. There's jazz on Fridays. "There are many, many people in our audience who have been coming to our concerts for thirty years because they love it. They are like part of the family," says Espina Ruiz. "Music really transforms us. It makes us go to places in our imagination, and we really feel replenished afterward." This is a great spot for folks of all abilities. Also make a stop to see the **Great**

Falls in Falls Village. The Housatonic River runs over a sixty-foot ledge, creating this visual and audible spectacle. Folks can even put a kayak in the bubbling whitewater area beneath the falls.

Norfolk: Sweet tunes are also abundant in Norfolk, a rustic town on the edge of the Berkshires. Every summer it hosts the **Norfolk Chamber Music Festival** (**www.music.yale.edu/norfolk**), part of the Yale Summer School of Music. "It was started in the early 1900s by a woman who was a wealthy music and arts benefactor named Ellen Battell Stoeckel. She had an estate in Norfolk and she loved music," says Melvin Chen, director of the festival, explaining that a music shed was erected on the property. "It's built out of California redwood that she had shipped here. The color and acoustics of the hall are quite striking and beautiful." While the music is classical, the vibe is casual, and all performances are held in the air-conditioned shed, which is accessible for all. Hear string quartets during nights dedicated to music legends like Stephen Sondheim and Benny Goodman. A series of weekend concerts from early July to mid-August feature professionals who come to Norfolk to teach. But remember: It's also a summer school with students. "During the concerts, you'll hear these world-renowned artists, but they're playing alongside the next generation of professional talent," says Chen, who loves this special combination. Visitors can also understand the process by watching open rehearsals. A yearly open house is free and family-friendly, inviting folks to events like a children's concert, an ice-cream social, and an art show.

Experience the sounds of both professional and emerging artists at the Norfolk Chamber Music Festival.
Sonja Zinke

And the musical destinations continue. Norfolk is also home to **Infinity Music Hall (www.infinityhall.com)**, an iconic destination in the state, with a companion location in Hartford. This intimate space houses more than two hundred shows each year. The venue was once an opera house, barbershop, and saloon back in the late 1880s. Then for years it was the home to vaudeville shows. Things changed, however, and the building was vacant for some time. It opened in its current capacity in 2007. Now the antiques details are accompanied by a first-rate sound system, modern amenities, and top-notch acts like 10,000 Maniacs, Jimmie Vaughn, and Ricky Scaggs. A variety of musical genres are presented here, including alternative rock, acoustic, bluegrass, blues, and classic rock. Infinity Hall offers accessibility for all patrons. This area also provides great hiking opportunities at **Dennis Hill State Park (portal.ct.gov/ DEEP/State-Parks/Parks/Dennis-Hill-State-Park)**, a former estate with a climb that takes visitors to a summit with fabulous views. **Haystack Mountain State Park (portal.ct.gov/DEEP/State-Parks/Parks/Haystack -Mountain-State-Park)** features another peaked climb. And **Campbell Falls State Park Reserve (portal.ct.gov/DEEP/State-Parks/Reserves/ Campbell-Falls-State-Park-Reserve)** is home to a gorgeous fifty-foot waterfall.

Norwalk: When the boys were really small, we lived in Fairfield, and my all-time favorite place to take them was the **Maritime Aquarium (www.maritime aquarium.org)**. It's set up like a big ramp. So when Sam was a toddler, he would cruise ahead of me, up and down the ramp, past the sea turtles, the octopus, and the otters. You know what would stop him in his tracks? The incredible, large blue tank filled with sand tiger sharks, a truly mesmerizing sight. Over the years we kept up a yearly visit to the aquarium as an exhibit filled

Kids will be transfixed by the shark tank and the large sea turtles at the Maritime Aquarium at Norwalk. The Maritime Aquarium

with adorable meerkats and an impressive ray touch tank were added to the mix. The aquarium also features a 4D theater and special educational and wildlife cruises aboard the R/V *Spirit of the Sound*. The aquarium is accessible for all, and families can request a sensory-friendly map at the entrance. The aquarium is located in a cool section of South Norwalk, affectionately called SoNo. So see marine life and then get a great lunch and

Tour the once-dilapidated Greens Ledge Lighthouse in Norwalk. Alexander Pettee

ice cream. Down the street, the **Norwalk Seaport Association (www .seaport.org)** offers boat tours May through September aboard a forty-five-foot catamaran. Visitors can head out on a three-hour adventure that includes a stop at the Sheffield Island Lighthouse. Interestingly, this lighthouse looks very similar to the Morgan Point Lighthouse, a privately owned home in Noank, along with Great Captain Island Light in Greenwich, all built around 1830. There has been a big push to restore and preserve the **Greens Ledge Lighthouse (ww.savegreensledge .org)**, built in 1902, off the coast of Norwalk. Tim Pettee and his family bought the spark plug–shaped beacon at auction in 2016 with the intention of sharing it with the public. "We want to make sure that the community is able to participate and visit and appreciate this great 120-year-old icon that had been sitting there for decades, boarded up, sealed up," he says, noting the generosity of many donors. "The local community has made this happen." The site features more than thirty thousand tons of rocks that came from the excavation of Radio City Music Hall. They help protect the island from the elements and boaters from the tough topography. "Until the light was put there, many boats ran aground on the ledge," says Pettee. "It's located a mile offshore and a mile west of the Norwalk Islands." For years, visitors were not allowed on the island, but today limited public and private tours are offered from late spring through early fall, with the cooperation of the Maritime Aquarium. Another great spot for kids in this culturally rich area is **Stepping Stones Museum for Children (www.steppingstonesmuseum.org)**,

Go back in time at Stepping Stones Museum for Children, sporting a dinosaur exhibit that's sure to delight.

renovated and updated during the pandemic. "At Stepping Stones, play-based learning takes place every day. We always say, "'Play is serious business,'" says Robert Townes, director of public affairs. The young boys and girls will love the animatronic Dilophosaurus, the Connecticut state dinosaur, along with a prehistoric exhibit that includes a pretend time machine and a paleontology-inspired dig site. Also check out an interactive television studio where young journalists can try their hand at presenting the weather or traffic report. The *Lights On* exhibit features a giant Lite-Brite, fun for kids and adults alike. And always a big hit, the Energy Lab, will soon be transformed into a space called The Biosphere, where small scientists can get a little wet learning about power in The Waterfall, The Water Funnel, and The Waterfall Basin, which involves swirling colored balls. The museum turns twenty-five years old in 2025. "We're now at the place in our history where we're starting to see Stepping Stones kids become Stepping Stones parents and bring their kids back," says Townes. "As a parent, there's nothing more exciting than seeing the world through your child's eyes." The museum is fully accessible and encourages visitation from those of all abilities and backgrounds. "All children deserve access to learning opportunities," says Townes of the Open Arms program that enables underserved children to utilize the museum at no cost. Right next to Stepping Stones find a historic vibe at the **Lockwood-Mathews Mansion Museum (www .lockwoodmathewsmansion.com)**. This sprawling house, a National

Historic Landmark, was built by railroad executive LeGrand Lockwood from 1864 to 1868. It is considered one of the first Second Empire country homes in the country. In the 1960s, passionate area residents saved the mansion from the threat of demolition. Guided tours show off an early central heating system that was considered new technology at the time, along with a fascinating look at servants' quarters, evoking comparisons to Downton Abbey, across the pond. The museum sports an elevator and ADA-compliant restrooms.

Milford: This city on the water is absolutely bustling in the summertime with a variety of shops, restaurants, and seventeen miles of shoreline. In the summer of 2022, a new attraction burst onto the scene in a big way. **Pedal Cruise CT (www.pedalcruise.com/connecticut/)** takes folks out of Milford Harbor into Long Island Sound for a unique outing that's all about socializing, sightseeing, and pedaling! That's right; it's a similar concept to Elm City Party Bike, founded by the same local

Take a group of friends out for a fun excursion on the water with Pedal Cruise CT. Pedal Cruise CT

entrepreneur. "The feeling of pedaling is maybe not as important on the boat. The access to water is what I think has excited people about Pedal Cruise," says Colin Caplan, who says he took hundreds of passengers out on this popular offering during the first summer. "It's one of the best opportunities for people to get out on the water in a group setting where you can relax with friends, enjoy some beverages and a snack, and pedal if you want to, make the paddle wheel move or just watch the birds and the sunset." Passengers can try their hand at steering the pontoon boat, which came from Florida. "Connecticut people know how to have fun," he says. A life jacket is required for children under the age of twelve. The city of Stamford also has a Pedal Cruise boat. Regarding access to Connecticut's shoreline, folks can visit **Silver Sands State Park (portal.ct.gov/DEEP/State-Parks/Parks/Silver-Sands-State-Park)**, which features the longest boardwalk in the state and is accessible for those of all abilities. Wheelchairs are available to borrow at the park. Look for beautiful seashells or birds, which are abundant in the area. To that point, take your binoculars to the **Connecticut Audubon Coastal Center (www.ctaudubon.org/coastal-center-home/)**, a nature center and bird sanctuary, open since 1995. Hundreds of species of birds have been spotted at this scenic location with fantastic views. The center offers wheelchairs designed for use on the beach, as well as a ramp to the beach. Every summer in mid-August, attend the **Milford Oyster Festival (www.milfordoysterfestival.com)**. In addition to thirty thousand oysters, enjoy music groups, a classic car show, kids activities, and even a kayak race! And for a unique experience, head to **Kinship Glassworks (www.kinship glassworks.com)**, a glassblowing studio where you can try your hand at this incredible art. The studio is accessible for those in a wheelchair.

Learn the art of glassblowing at Kinship Glassworks in Milford.

Portland: Seeking adventurous fun that's sure to tire out the kiddos? Look no further than **Brownstone Adventure Sports Park (www .brownstonepark.com)**, a supercool place, no pun intended. It opened in 2006, and just continues to grow. What used to be a run-down relic, where daredevils trespassed to swim surreptitiously in the forbidden quarry, is now an action-packed arena of fun, featuring rock climbing, cliff jumping, wakeboarding, kayaking, and of course zip lining, a main attraction. Soar across the park on a vast array of lines. You can even try out snorkeling and zip lining in the quarry, which is an incredibly cool place with eighty-five-foot solid brownstone walls and a depth of one hundred feet. The brownstone found here was used in the construction of buildings in cities such as Boston, Chicago, and New Haven. The site is a National Historic Landmark and is also listed on the National Register of Historic Places. This destination is known to get teens off their electronics to try

Soar through the air, swim, and jump off ledges at super-adventurous Brownstone Adventure Sports Park.

out new experiences alongside Mom and Dad. Truth be told, my husband and I always act like big kids when we're there. Soar down a waterslide, climb a giant inflatable iceberg, or have your child launch you off a giant blob! You won't be sorry. Sports activities are recommended for kids ages eight and up. Brownstone is happy to work with anyone with a disability to figure out how they can best use the park. Those in wheelchairs must navigate through a small beach to enter the park. This fun spot is open Memorial Day through Labor Day. For a relaxing day in Portland, head to the **Arrigoni Winery** (**www.arrigoniwinery.com**), near the Arrigoni Bridge. This bucolic destination hosts tastings of a variety of wines. "The vineyard is a 280-acre farm that's family owned. The vibe is just a cool, fun place to hang out. We have over five hundred seats outside with live music," says brand manager Rosanna Singer, noting that the vineyard

is open Friday, Saturday, and Sunday. "We have over thirty different labels of wine. It's a great time." In addition to wine and wine slushies, the winery offers designer-crafted hard ciders from different parts of New England. It's a family-friendly scene, and dogs on leashes are allowed on the grounds. No outside beverages can be brought in, including water, but you can bring a picnic. Arrigoni, open

Sit by the vines and enjoy music, along with some great spirits, at Arrigoni Winery in Portland.

The Air Line State Park Trail stretches through several towns, including Portland and East Hampton.

since 2012, offers some food, such as flatbreads, along with crackers and cheese. This location is ADA compliant. The **Air Line State Park Trail (portal.ct.gov/DEEP/State-Parks/Parks/Air-Line-State-Park-Trail)** is a great resource for outdoor enjoyment. This old train line, once the route between New York to Boston, stretches through several towns in eastern Connecticut, including Portland, East Hampton, Lebanon, Pomfret, and Thompson. This linear trail is a piece of state history, dating back to the late 1800s, but it also affords great opportunities for walkers, bikers, and even horseback riders. Folks in wheelchairs can utilize some sections of the trail in East Hampton, Colchester, and Hebron.

Madison: Going out on a limb here, but I'm willing to say that **Hammonasset Beach State Park (portal.ct.gov/DEEP/State-Parks/Parks/Hammonasset-Beach-State-Park)** is one of the most special spots in the state, drawing an astounding three million people to the

Hammonasset Beach State Park offers visitors several beautiful beaches along with rocky walks, perfect for exploration.

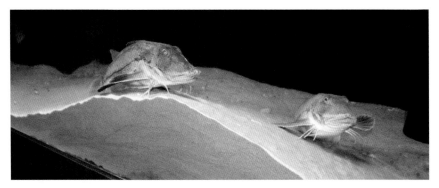

The newly built Meigs Point Nature Center offers a great reprieve from the sun and views of critters from our surroundings.

park each year. It's considered the largest of the state's shoreline parks and offers several gorgeous beaches for swimming and fishing. It's a popular spot for camping mid-May to Columbus Day. Find boardwalks for strolling and picnic areas for eating away from the sand. This park is accessible and even sports several beach wheelchairs that visitors can borrow. After some time at the beach, take the kids to the **Meigs Point Nature Center (www.meigspointnaturecenter.org)**, close to all the beaches. This new, fully accessible, four-thousand-square-foot state-of-the-art building opened in 2016. The center houses four sections: "In the Air," "In the Woods," "In the Water," and "At the Beach." Most of all, kids will love to see the real-life critters, such as snakes, frogs, and turtles, on display. And coming from the mom of two boys, a touch tank never disappoints! "The advantage of our nature center is that it focuses on native wildlife. So it's things that you can see or encounter in the state of Connecticut and mostly things you're going to see at Hammonasset Beach State Park. We're really trying to keep the focus on Long Island Sound, the beach, and the salt marshes," explains Russ Miller, who helps maintain this popular center. There's a great recreational path right near Hammonasset, courtesy of the **Shoreline Greenway Trail (www .shorelinegreenwaytrail.org)**. This ambitious project aims to connect communities in a twenty-five-mile corridor from Madison to New Haven. The paved path accommodates walkers, runners, bikers, and folks in wheelchairs. The trail is not yet complete. The Madison stretch stands at 1.1 miles, leading visitors past marshlands and over a bridge, allowing for gorgeous views. From nature to culture, take a stroll through Madison's incredible downtown area, filled with fantastic restaurants and shops, including a well-known independent bookstore, **R.J. Julia**

Booksellers (www.rjjulia.com). Don't miss the chance to walk through the **Sculpture Mile (www.hollycroftfoundation.org/madison-ct-1)**, with more than twenty works by American artists nestled in interesting spots around Main Street. And for a dose of history, check out the **Allis-Bushnell House and Museum (www.madisonhistory.org/allis -bushnell-house/)**, dating back to the late 1700s, containing period furniture and listed on the National Register of Historic Places. Museum guides tell fascinating stories of life from colonial times, through the Revolutionary and Civil Wars, to the Colonial Revival period. The first floor is accessible to all visitors. Exploration of this destination includes a walk through the beautiful gardens and a look inside a shed at old tools and other artifacts.

Middlebury: Quassy Amusement & Waterpark (www.quassy.com) really hits all the buttons for a fun summer outing. "We are a family amusement park, celebrating our 115th year of operation here in Connecticut," says co-owner George Frantzis. "We have all the fun things a big amusement park has but with a lot more intimacy on twenty acres of lakefront property." Amusement park rides such as the swinging chairs and the Tilt-A-Whirl allow for classic entertainment, while the award-winning Wooden Warrior roller coaster provides the real thrills. All in all,

Enjoy the classic rides and waterpark at Quassy Amusement & Waterpark in Middlebury. Quassy Amusement & Waterpark

find more than twenty rides. Some are even appropriate for little kids. But during those inevitable heat waves, it's the Splash Away Bay Waterpark that appeals to fun seekers. Get drenched by the giant bucket of water, officially called the Saturation Station, or try the tunnel twister slides. For the older kids, grab a raft and cruise down the BulletBowl slide, full of twists and turns. A fairly new attraction, the Rocket Rapids Water Coaster, is the first of its kind in the state. Hold your breath or let out the shrieks as the coaster dips and takes on sharp turns. I recently rode it with my good friend Maeve, and we had tons of fun. This destination also offers an arcade, picnicking, and occasional live entertainment. My dear friend with special needs absolutely loves her summer days at Quassy, which overlooks beautiful Lake Quassapaug. Frantzis says the park works with many kids with autism to make sure they are comfortable, and will help their families avoid long lines. Most of the park is accessible for those in wheelchairs.

Bristol: Searching for classic summer fun? Look no further than **Lake Compounce (www.lakecompounce.com)**, opened in 1848 and considered the oldest continuously operating amusement park in North America. "People have this nostalgic feeling when they visit the park. Although we've made a lot of updates in recent years, we always get comments from people saying they remember when they visited as a kid and now they're bringing their kids back to the park. It really is a beloved spot that holds a special place in a lot of Connecticut residents' hearts. It's fun. There are lots of happy memories here," says Lynsey Winters, communications director for Palace Entertainment, which runs the park. "We have Connecticut's largest waterpark. In the summertime, that's where most people spend their time." With fun for all ages, the roller coasters have a loyal fan base. "In 2016 we added Phobia, the first

Visit Connecticut's largest waterpark and sample the roller coasters at Lake Compounce in Bristol. Lake Compounce Amusement Park

triple-launch coaster in New England. It's definitely for thrill seekers. I'd say it's our most intense attraction in the park," says Winters, also highlighting more family-friendly rides like the Wildcat Coaster. "Then we have the Boulder Dash, which has been voted Best Wooden Roller Coaster in the World five times. People fly from all over the world to ride Boulder Dash." Also find a carousel, trolley rides, bumper cars, and a Ferris wheel. Wheelchairs and scooters are available for folks to rent. For safety reasons, riders must be able to maintain proper riding position for each attraction. Lake Compounce provides extensive information on accessibility on its website. Interesting fact: Milli Vanilli's infamous lip-synching gaffe took place at Lake Compounce in 1989. The city of Bristol also contains several quirky and interesting museums. The **New England Carousel Museum (www.thecarouselmuseum.org)** is a thirty-three-thousand-square-foot building containing one hundred years of history pertaining to the classic spinning rides. See unique carved horses and even a section dedicated to the history of firefighting. The museum is accessible for those with mobility issues. The **American Clock and Watch Museum (www.clockandwatchmuseum.org)** tells the significance of Connecticut's role in the clock and watch industries through a self-guided tour. Stroll through eight galleries to see items such as sundials and unique character watches. Kids can take part in a scavenger hunt. Most of the museum is accessible for all visitors. Also check out **Imagine Nation, A Museum Early Learning Center (www .imaginenation.org)**, offering family programming in topics such as art and science by reservation only. The building is fully accessible.

Canterbury: There's an important site in this charming rural town that deserves a stop for reflection. It's the **Prudence Crandall Museum (portal.ct.gov/DECD/Content/Historic-Preservation/04_State _Museums/Prudence-Crandall-Museum/Plan-Your-Visit)**, named for Connecticut's State Heroine, a woman who fought for social justice way ahead of her time. "The museum is the actual site of the Canterbury Female Boarding School. We are a National Historic Landmark and archaeological preserve in Canterbury. We are also part of the Last Green Valley," explains Joanie DiMartino, museum curator and site superintendent. (Learn more about the Last Green Valley in our "Killingly" section.) At first Crandall's school served only white students. But in 1832 a black woman named Sarah Harris asked Crandall if she could attend as well. When Crandall accepted her into the classrooms, townspeople protested the integration of the school. "She closed her school down to white students and reopened on April 1st of 1833 for black and brown students," says DiMartino, noting that students then came from all around the region. "The town and state responded with both intimidation and harassment. People threw eggs and rocks at the school." Crandall was arrested and faced legal problems. Then a mob attack shut down the entire operation. While the school was open only eighteen months, it left an enormous impact. "It was short-lived, but it

Left: Learn all about Connecticut's State Heroine, Prudence Crandall, who created a school for black students.
Right: The CT 169 corridor is designated a scenic route by the state and features stops on the Wine Trail.

was a success. The students went on to do incredible things in activism and education. They were leaders in their communities," says DiMartino. "Prudence Crandall is the State Heroine not only because of what she did but also because of what she inspired us to continue to do." Open May through October, the museum shows visitors a story that is still relevant today, and it exposes Connecticut's sometimes unknown history of racial inequality. "While the students that attended school here were free, they were not considered equal," says DiMartino. The museum recently underwent a major restoration, which included a new ADA-compliant ramp and other updates. Head to the website for information about timed tours. The house sits on the CT 169 corridor, designated a "scenic road" by the State of Connecticut. "Back in the day, it was an indigenous pathway and later part of the Underground Railroad, with several hosts along the way," says Jill St. Clair of the **Eastern Regional Tourism District (portal.ct.gov/DECD/Content/Tourism/06_About_Tourism Office/Eastern-Regional-Tourism-District**), noting that a ride down this roadway affords great views of old homes, antique barns, and green farmlands. The **Quinebaug River**, offering opportunities for kayaking and eagle watching, runs parallel to CT 169. "There are several public launch areas, one under the bridge connecting Canterbury to Plainfield on CT 14. The gentle river winds six miles to the Butts Bridge launch site," says St. Clair. "Butts Bridge is a Depression-era public works steel bridge, a fantastic piece of industrial art that is photographic gold."

East Lyme: Find a little bit of everything during a summer trip to East Lyme, which includes the village of Niantic. Take a stroll around beautiful **Rocky Neck State Park (portal.ct.gov/DEEP/State-Parks/Parks/Rocky -Neck-State-Park)**, a lovely beach with views of train tracks for kids (like my Sam) who love to see those locomotives chugging along the tracks.

The lovely beach off the Niantic Bay Boardwalk includes features for those of all abilities.

This is also a great, gentle area for swimming or crabbing. This accessible park offers beach wheelchairs if needed. Toward the center of town, find **Niantic Bay Beach (eltownhall.com/ government/departments/ parks-recreation/parks/cini -memorial-park-beach/)**, which is accessible for those of all abilities; a mat on a patch of sand leads to the water using an on-site wheelchair. The beach is a half mile long, with access to an incredible boardwalk that's open to the public—a really special area, perfect for a vigorous scenic stroll featuring fantastic views and a wonderful sea breeze. Dogs, bikes, and skateboards are not permitted on the boardwalk. The **Niantic Children's Museum (www.nianticchildrensmuseum .org)**, an interactive, hands-on spot for young kids, offers an Imagination Room along with a

Rocky Neck State Park offers a lovely beach experience along with views of trains.

Discovery Room. The **Book Barn** (**www.bookbarnniantic.com**), called "a Bibliophile's Bliss," is a charming place for those who love to turn the pages. Think 350,000 gently-used books, sometimes stacked floor to ceiling. Longtime employees and adorable cats roam freely around the multi-building location, which includes outdoor kiosks. This is also a great place to sell the books you're ready to give up. Keep the cultural vibe going with a stop at the **Samuel Smith Farmstead** (**samuelsmithfarmstead.org**), showing life on a colonial farm. "The land has been farmed since

Find a gem of a story or sell your gently-used titles at Niantic's Book Barn.

1685. The house on the property was built in two stages during the years 1720 and 1740. We offer tours of the house," explains Benn Bullock, president of the Friends of Samuel Smith House, which maintains the property. There's a barn, also built around 1720, that folks can peruse, plus seventeen acres of lovely fields and farmland. This site, on the Connecticut State Historic Preservation Commission and the National Register of Historic Places, is open Sundays from Memorial Day through Labor Day. It also hosts special events in the summertime, such as a vintage truck and tractor show, an open-farm day, and a Revolutionary War–era encampment. Bullock says that it's a special place where some visitors bird-watch, stroll through gardens, or traverse a walking path. "People are just now beginning to find it and enjoy it. Some folks come out just for peace and quiet," he says. A visit here is free, although donations are accepted. Each June the state hosts Connecticut Historic House Day. The farmstead is not accessible for those in wheelchairs.

Experience life on a colonial farm at the charming Samuel Smith Farmstead.

Old Saybrook: I simply love this town. It's got tons of great attributes, but my number-one reason for adoring Old Saybrook will always revolve around **Harvey's Beach (www.oldsaybrookct.myrec.com/ info/facilities/details.aspx?FacilityID=8306**). While the Old Saybrook

coastline includes some private community beaches and Town Beach, just for residents, out-of-towners can pay a fee at Harvey's and get right in. Find lifeguards, restrooms, and changing rooms. That said, it does fill up on beautiful summer days, especially at low tide, when the incredible area opens into a large expanse, perfect for long walks and playing Frisbee with the kids after making a sandcastle. It's glorious. "We have people that come and enjoy the beaches, fishing, and swimming," says Judy Sullivan, executive director of the **Old**

Saybrook Point Miniature Golf provides family fun and stunning views of the area where the Connecticut River meets Long Island Sound.

Saybrook Chamber of Commerce (www.oldsaybrookchamber .com), noting that the Amtrak station brings regular visitors into town from New York and Boston. "Sunsets are always beautiful. You'll see a lot of people out there around sunset time with their cameras. It never gets old." Visitors can spend a day at the beach then drive over a well-known causeway with views of Fenwick, a private community where legendary actress Katharine Hepburn lived for years. The causeway

ends near **Saybrook Point Miniature Golf** (oldsaybrookct .myrec.com/info/facilities/ details.aspx?FacilityID=8307), perfect for family fun; it's open May through Columbus Day weekend. The course, which takes about an hour to complete, is super fun, featuring lighthouses and local landmarks dotting the greenway. It's part of **Saybrook Point Park**, which boasts

Nothing beats the sunset at Harvey's Beach in Old Saybrook at low tide.

118

incredible views of the area where the Connecticut River meets Long Island Sound. Nearby, find **Fort Saybrook Monument Park**, an eighteen-acre stretch with signage that explains the history of the area, one of the state's oldest towns, founded in 1635. A boardwalk attracts birders. In 1980 many artifacts from Native Americans and early European settlers were found in the area during archaeological exploration. Find an homage to Fort Saybrook, the first military post built on the Connecticut River, also the site of battle during the Pequot War. See a statue of Lion Gardner, an engineer and soldier who designed

Learn about Old Saybrook's founding father and early history at Fort Saybrook Monument Park.

the fort in the 1600s, along with a layout for the town. The Connecticut Valley Railroad had a roundhouse and end-of-the-line turntable from the late 1870s on this site. Relics from this time are still visible. This park is ADA compliant. Continue a drive into the lovely downtown area, home to a variety of shops and eateries, along with a spot that's become a cultural mecca. "**The Kate (www.katharinehepburntheater.org**) is definitely a huge draw, bringing tens of thousands of people into town each year," says Sullivan of the 250-seat accessible cultural center named for Hepburn, which each year shows a bevy of musical concerts, all styles ranging from rock to pop to Broadway fare. "We also have a historic walking tour here at the chamber of commerce. It takes you from one end of Main Street down to the other. It's self-guided thanks to a paper pamphlet, and it explains all the old homes. People love it." No pun intended, the **Lucky 33 Gemstone Flume Mine** is a hidden gem in Old Saybrook. When they were ages five to ten, say, my sons absolutely loved this small location where kids could use a flume to mine for treasures. The owner, filled with knowledge, cuts and polishes stones on-site. For a small fee, kids can bring their finds home. Here's a perk: This shop is right across the street from Dairy Queen! The **Preserve (oldsaybrookct .myrec.com/info/facilities/details.aspx?FacilityID=11630**), made up

Get a view of the Saybrook Breakwater Lighthouse, marking the channel at the mouth of the Connecticut River.

of parts of Essex, Westbrook, and Old Saybrook, is a well-known hiking spot, recognized as the largest remaining unprotected coastal forest between New York and Boston. Lastly, if you're lucky enough to catch a cruise around Old Saybrook's beautiful coast, be sure to take pictures of the **Lynde Point Light**, the town's "inner lighthouse," and **Saybrook Breakwater Lighthouse**, it's "outer" companion, marking the channel at the mouth of the Connecticut River. You can also get a glimpse of Katharine Hepburn's stately home, not far from the lighthouse.

Westbrook: For nonresidents, here are some tips for enjoying the shoreline in this beautiful town. The **Stewart B. McKinney National Wildlife Refuge (www.fws.gov/refuge/stewart-b-mckinney)** includes Westbrook. This federally owned and protected area provides habitat for birds and reptiles. "It's five hundred acres of salt marsh that meanders up north of us," says Gene Chmiel, owner of **Black Hall Outfitters (www.blackhalloutfitters.com)**, a paddle sport center, located on the preserve and the Menunketesuck River Kayak Trail, renting out kayaks and stand-up paddleboards. Simply jump in your single or tandem craft and set off to enjoy all the beauty this area has to offer. "It's protected, shallow, calm waters that do not have heavy boat traffic or heavy tidal influence," says Chmiel, noting that this is considered one of the "epic" paddling destinations in the Northeast. Participants can see Duck Island

Visit the gorgeous Water's Edge Resort & Spa in Westbrook for a holiday brunch and a stroll on the beach.

and Menunketesuck, both bird sanctuaries. Folks can also learn about this special area by booking an adventure in the salty Long Island Sound with **Joy Ride Charters (www.joyridecharters.com)** from May through October. "I offer sailing charters, day charters, to people looking to celebrate or people who like being on the water, whether it's to pop the question or just get out with family," says Captain Joy Sherman, who offers hourly, half-day, or full-day excursions on a fully staffed Catalina 36 sailboat. "It is an expensive hobby for people. I really love that I can offer this to people on a budget who may want to figure out if they like sailing or just want to get out on the water to try it." Sherman, who has lived in Connecticut her whole life, talks to passengers about taking care of our waters, along with the importance of wearing sunscreen and sunglasses. "I love to take advantage of our Connecticut coastline, which is fantastic. Some of the best sailing in the world is right here in Connecticut, I think, and I've sailed everywhere," she says. Sherman says her boat cannot accommodate wheelchairs, but with assistance, the crew can get people on board and into the cockpit safely. There are two steps to the deck level. Then there's always the glorious **Water's Edge Resort & Spa (www .watersedgeresortandspa.com)**, accessible for all, offering fantastic brunches, lunches, and dinners. After their meal, visitors can wander down to the property's beach, pull up a beach chair, and enjoy incredible views. At low tide, folks can walk or kayak out to Salt Island, visible from the shore. But beware! It's not unusual for people to get stuck out there when the tide comes in.

Clinton: Next door, find more of the same vibe in Clinton, where there are some great opportunities for enjoying Connecticut's coastline. Once the Memorial Day parade kicks off, Clinton regains its status as a summer town, with much of the action revolving around the shoreline. **Blue Fin Charters (www.bluefincharters.com)** gets folks out for a half- or full-day adventure, fishing for striped bass, bluefish, fluke, porgy, and blackfish. Folks can go out even farther to search for sharks, tuna, marlin, and more. Find a similar scenario at **Rock & Roll Charters (www.rock androllcharters.com)**. "We go out seven days a week and offer morning trips and afternoon trips," says owner T. J. Karbowski. "Out of almost the entire Eastern Seaboard, we have some of the calmest waters." The boat

Take a fishing trip with Rock & Roll Charters and return home with stripers or blackfish. T. J. Karbowski

holds a group of six people. Most, but not all, participants are Connecticut residents looking to have a turnkey fishing excursion. "We do have world-class fishing over here. We have some of the best striped bass fishing anywhere because we are right on the striped bass migration route. We really are a hidden gem that nobody knows about," says Karbowski. The boat cannot accommodate a wheelchair, but plenty of seniors with walkers have been passengers. There are no stairs to board, and the entrance of the boat is flush with the dock. In addition to the fishing opportunities, Clinton is a vibrant town full of great shops and spots for foodies. "We have a town marina with a few restaurants; one is nationally known, **Lobster Landing (www.lobsterlandingct.com)**," says Paul Orsini, executive director of the Clinton Chamber of Commerce, referring

Find a high-end bargain at Clinton Premium Outlets, a shopping attraction in Clinton.

to a beloved eatery with great food and ambience. "We have summer concerts on The Green on Thursday nights. We have several large festivals." Out-of-towners can go to Clinton's lovely Town Beach, with a fantastic playground and splash pad for kids. But beware! Prepare for a large price tag. "The Saturday before Labor Day, we have one of the biggest fireworks and summer festival displays in Connecticut," says Orsini, adding that nonresidents are welcome. Shopping is big in this town, as it's home to the **Clinton Premium Outlets** (**www.premium outlets.com/outlet/clinton**), featuring items from Nike, Ralph Lauren, Ann Taylor, and much more. Folks can even rent wheelchairs in the management office. Switching gears to history, check out the **Adam Stanton House & General Store** (**www.adamstantonhouse.org**), built in 1791. The home is still filled with original items like wallpaper and furniture that belonged to the Stanton family, who operated a general store in the 1800s. Visitors can still see original documents and inventory, providing a real look at life during colonial times. Free tours can be arranged by contacting the home. Donations are encouraged. Guides can put together special tours for those with developmental disabilities. But due to the historic nature of the buildings, they are not wheelchair accessible. **Chamard Vineyards** (**www.chamard.com**) has become a popular destination in the state. Opened in the late 1980s, the forty-acre property yields Cabernet Franc, Cabernet Sauvignon, Chardonnay, Merlot, and Pinot Noir grapes. Visitors enjoy the vibe, both casual and elegant, while relaxing in the sun on the grounds or sampling farm-to-table food in the Bistro. This destination is ADA compliant.

Lyme: This quiet rural community boasts both dense woodlands and beautiful coastline along the Connecticut River. One of its most unique assets is **Selden Neck State Park (portal.ct.gov/DEEP/State-Parks/ Parks/Selden-Neck-State-Park)**, an island that broke away from the mainland in the 1850s. In the 1880s it served as a quarry of red granite schist, used for paving stones. Today folks can take a boat to the uninhabited 607-acre island for an adventure, exploring the trails, looking for wildlife, and enjoying incredible views of the river. **Hamburg Cove** is a well-known destination for boaters, who often hook up to a mooring and spend an afternoon swimming and relaxing in this charming area. The lovely cove is surrounded by antique colonial homes. At **Cove Landing Marine (www.covelanding.com)**, rent a sailboat, a kayak, or a stand-up paddleboard to take into the cove to see the sites and get exercise, all at the same time. "There's so much wildlife. It's just

Rent a sailboat, kayak, or stand-up paddleboard at Cove Landing Marine in Hamburg Cove.

an untouched, beautiful, quiet cove area that's not really disturbed or developed. It's just a quiet place to bring a bagged lunch then go and explore what nature has to offer in this hidden gem," says Jen Leonard, owner of Cove Landing Marine, who says people love to visit the area to see owls or eagles. "There's a pretty good chance you're going to run into something pretty fabulous out there." The marina also rents out moorings so folks can experience a day or an overnight in the cove that features brackish water—part fresh, part salt—due to its proximity to the

See farm animals in a relaxed atmosphere and shop for specialty foods at Sankow's Beaver Brook Farm.

mouth of the river into Long Island Sound. Also make a stop at **Sankow's Beaver Brook Farm (www.beaverbrookfarm.com)** to witness life on a working farm. "We are not a petting zoo. What we have are animals in their natural setting. We have cows and sheep," says owner Suzanne Sankow, noting that families love to see lambs in the spring and early summer. "They play. They run back and forth and jump straight up. They show so much joy." The farm is well-known for its homemade cheeses and prepared food, including a stuffed chicken that's become very popular. Visitors in wheelchairs can navigate the farm. Folks can also take a beautiful walk at **Becket Hill State Park Reserve (portal.ct.gov/ DEEP/State-Parks/Locate-Park-Forest/Other-State-Parks-and-Forests #BecketHill)** or **Nehantic State Forest (portal.ct.gov/DEEP/State -Parks/Forests/Nehantic-State-Forest)**, also a spot for swimming, boating, letterboxing, and picnicking.

Montville: On a rainy day, there's an awesome spot for the whole family. **Supercharged (www.superchargedracing.com)** is an emporium of fun, located in a huge industrial park–like setting off a main drag. We hosted one of my son's birthday parties at this venue, and I gotta say, no one will complain or go home bored. Head to what's called the World's Largest Indoor Multi-Level Karting Track with zippy electric,

Find hours of family fun, including indoor go-karting and axe throwing, at Supercharged in Montville.

zero-emission karts. Don a helmet and take the wheel as you embark on races with fellow participants. It certainly gets the adrenaline going and is a whole lot of fun. Supercharged sports a Ninja Wipeout obstacle course with a net maze, cave crawl, and more. And trampolines and arcade games never disappoint. Finally, for those age fifteen and over, axe throwing is on the agenda. Safety measures are strict as folks grip the axe, place it behind their heads, and throw toward an interactive projection target for competitive fun. It's certainly a stress release and a unique activity. The Axe Lounge features food and drinks, as does V's Brick Oven Pizzeria & Pub. The building is wheelchair accessible. There is even a special kart, operated by hand controls, that can be driven by someone with mobility issues. Patrons should call and reserve it in advance. And if you're driving through this area, you can't miss Monty the Dinosaur, overlooking CT 85 and drawing families into a seriously fun and special place, **Nature's Art Village** (**www.naturesartvillage.com**). And speaking of birthday parties, we hosted a joint celebration for my sons at this destination when they were turning three and five, respectively. What an awesome, awesome spot, filled with a "village" of fun spots that seem to go on and on. Let's start with the **Dinosaur Place**, where you can stroll through more than 1.5 miles of ADA-compliant nature trails that aren't paved but are wide and smooth. The trail winds around a scenic lake and features more than sixty life-size dinosaurs to discover. The Brachiosaurus measures seventy-five feet long by forty feet tall! My sons loved to play in the SpaceNet, a one-of-a-kind playground structure. Don't get lost in a maze where folks can play then slide out through the mouth of a T-rex. During the summer, visitors can don a bathing suit and run around the Splash Pad, another giant hit with my sons. We made a point to go there every summer to stand under the giant bucket that gradually fills up, then drenches delighted children below. We would wrap up with an ice cream on the way home. Perfection. As they got older, we also frequented

Monty the T-Rex welcomes visitors to the Dinosaur Place in Montville, with a 1.5-mile nature trail and more than 60 life-size dinos.

the Copper Creek Mini Golf, an automatic good time. This location also offers an indoor Discovery Depot, where kids can dig for gems and pan for gold. If that's not enough, you can visit the Genius Museum, open Saturday and Sunday afternoons. The museum showcases the transformation of American technology over two centuries. "For instance, learn about the evolution of phones, typewriters, clocks, cameras, vinyl phonographs, barbershop equipment, washing machines, printing presses, farming, steam engines, gas engines, and even dental equipment," says Daniel Kornegay, marketing director for Nature's Art Village. "Older adults often feel nostalgic, and the young will learn how everyday life has developed with technological advances. It's a fully guided tour; we have a curator there who will take people around."

The Splash Pad at the Dinosaur Place offers a cooldown after a fun day of activities.

Canton/Collinsville: Collinsville is a quaint village in Canton that is really one of the most charming, scenic spots in the state. The village, complete with antiques shops and great restaurants, is on the Farmington River, offering an abundance of recreation for nature lovers. "We're right on the river where it's been dammed up, so it's a great area to paddle. There's a little bit of current, really beautiful scenery, and tons of wildlife," says Sue Warner, owner of **Collinsville Canoe & Kayak** (**www.collinsvillecanoe.com**), which has been in business for thirty-three years, renting kayaks, stand-up paddleboards, and more. "We also

Rent a kayak, canoe, or paddleboard at Collinsville Canoe & Kayak, in a beautiful section of the Farmington River.

rent out a big giant paddleboard that people love going on." This area offers a literal treasure trove of outdoor activities. The shop also rents bikes for people to use on the **Farmington Canal Heritage Trails**, which run for 56 miles, and the **Farmington River Trail** (**www.fchtrail .org**), spanning eighteen miles and called one of the most picturesque and historic greenways in the region. Due to its value in the area, the FCHT has been designated a Community Millenium Trail under the federal Millenium Trails program. Don't miss a stop at the **Roaring Brook Nature Center** (**www.roaringbrook.org**), full of activities for the kids. Inside the center, see small animals like rabbits, snakes, a leopard gecko, a bearded dragon, turtles, frogs, and even cockroaches! Outside, find more than one hundred acres with hiking trails, native plants, and opportunities to see wildlife. The center features special programming

The Farmington River Trail provides a safe and scenic pathway for bikers.

like nature walks and concerts for families throughout the year. The building is wheelchair accessible, as are some small nature trails.

Fairfield: When we got engaged, we bought a little yellow Cape with a white picket fence in this beautiful town, and I thought it was absolutely the best spot I had ever seen. For seven years we enjoyed this vibrant area with its gorgeous beaches and busy restaurants. Close to our home, we often strolled through the **Fairfield University Art Museum (www .fairfield.edu/museum)**. The beautiful galleries hold a variety of styles, including Medieval, Celtic, and Asian art, along with various changing exhibits on topics such as human rights and women artists. The museum is accessible for those of all abilities. For a natural experience, head to the **Connecticut Audubon Society Center (www.ctaudubon.org/ fairfield-home)**, a wildlife sanctuary and nature center in the beautiful Greenfield Hills section of town, featuring 155 acres with 7 miles of incredible trails that offer great opportunities for birding. The Edna Strube Chiboucas Special Use Trail is a one-mile jaunt, accessible for strollers and wheelchairs. The center has an indoor component as well, with small animals such as turtles and hamsters on display. "We also have our aviary, which features seven birds of prey. Those are on display for education about raptors and are used in programs as well," says Amy Barnouw, director of the Fairfield Region for the Connecticut Audubon Society. "People get to come and have this wonderful up-close and personal experience, often for the first time, with owls, hawks, and

See incredible birds that can't be released into the wild at the Connecticut Audubon Society Center in Fairfield.

a kestrel. We have really beautiful animals. They're extremely well cared for and well loved. Many people in the community know them by name and have visited them for years and years." The Audubon Society has a second location, closer to downtown, called the **Birdcraft Center**. "It's a really wonderful little gem," says Barnouw, noting that it dates back to 1914. "It's the first songbird sanctuary in the United States and it's on the National Register of Historic Places." But my favorite thing about Fairfield is access to the incredible beaches. I spent so much time there when the boys were little. We would swing, dig, and wander through the racks of kayaks, using them to teach the little guys about colors. **Fairfield beaches (www.fairfieldct.org/content/2765/2783/3417.aspx)** are open to the public (nonresidents), but entrance fees are pricey. Let's start with Penfield and Jennings, both along the same strip. They're lovely beaches, great for walking and running around with kids, especially during low tide. Jennings—at twenty-seven acres, the largest Fairfield beach—is accessible for folks of all abilities. It also sports a skate park and a fantastic Sand Castle Playground, where my boys would play for hours and hours. It's very well done, providing tons of fun. Southport is a section of Fairfield. When I tell you that a trip to the Southport beaches feels like a vacation, I'm not kidding. Sasco Beach is at the end of Sasco Hill Road, an incredible stretch with classic brick mansions and a swanky country club. But the beach is quaint and gorgeous, with a secluded, private feel. It's the perfect place to study hermit crabs with the kids or to enjoy date night while watching an incredible sunset. This beach is available to residents only from Memorial Day through Labor Day, but give it a go after-hours or during offseason months. You won't be sorry.

East Windsor: This town boasts an important historical location: the **Connecticut Trolley Museum (www.ct-trolley.org)**, considered the nation's oldest organization dedicated to the preservation of the trolley era. "We are a historic trolley transportation museum founded in 1940. We run historic trolleys that date back one hundred years," says executive director Gina Maria Alimberti. "You are taking a trip back in time by riding trolleys. You're not looking at a static display; you're experiencing it by actually taking a trip on the trolleys." During a three-mile excursion, see the sites and experience the feeling of transportation in the olden days. The museum recently received a grant to purchase and install a mobile wheelchair lift on the trolley, which is opening up new opportunities for people with mobility issues. In addition to a ride on the trolley, a stroll through the museum, also accessible, is valuable. "We have a full visitor center with static, real trolleys you can go inside and view.

MARC GLUCKSMAN
f RIVER RAIL PHOTO

The Connecticut Trolley Museum is the nation's oldest organization dedicated to the preservation of the trolley era.

We have a lot of hands-on exhibits. We do a lot with the kids. There's a Lego station, a craft station, and a dress-up station where kids can dress up like a motorman. It's a great photo op," says Alimberti. The nonprofit relies on special events, like Superhero & Princess Day, to help keep the museum going. There are also sensory-friendly days, dedicated to children with autism. "We're really gearing our museum toward families," says Alimberti. On-site, find the **Connecticut Fire Museum**, with a large display of antique apparatus dating back to the 1920s. The history continues with a fascinating area in the center of town: **Museums on the Green (www.eastwindsorhistory.com)**. Several historic museums and barns, within close proximity to one another, are available for

Left: The barbershop, built in 1891, was moved to this unique area. Right: The East Windsor Academy, built on this site in 1817, provided higher education for mostly boys.

viewing, thanks to the historical society. Open on Saturdays all year long, the campus includes a schoolhouse, a probate courthouse, a tobacco barn showcasing agricultural items, a barbershop, an academy from 1817, and the Osborn House, built in 1785. "So many people say, 'Wow, it's like a little Sturbridge Village,' only everything has come from East Windsor," says Nancy Masters, a volunteer with the historical society. There is a pathway down to the Scantic River for easy traversing. Additionally, there are ramps to the academy and Osborn House. Several other buildings are on ground level, with no stairs required to enter.

UNIQUE OUTINGS FOR SUMMER

Head to **CT AgFairs** (*www.ctagfairs.org*) for all information about Connecticut's vibrant fair scene! When my boys were little, we used to love to attend the **Chester Fair** (*www.chesterfair.org*), with classic amusement rides, large pretzels, even bigger stuffed animals, farm animals, and inflatable aliens (truth)! Other big fairs in the state include the **Bridgewater Country Fair** (*www.bridgewaterfair.com*), the **Hamburg Fair** (*www.hamburgfair.org*), and the **North Stonington Agricultural Fair** (*www.northstoningtonfair.org*).

Connecticut sports a robust fair season with corn dogs, animal shows, and classic rides! Berlin Fair

Or take an outing to see the **Dragon Boat and Asian Festival** (*www.riverfront.org/events/riverfront-asian-festival*) at **Mortensen Riverfront Plaza** (*www.riverfront.org/mortensen-riverfront-plaza/*) in Hartford, held each year in mid-August. Create a team or just head down to the river to buy some great food while watching the races, truly an incredible site. Dragon boat racing has been a pastime in China for two thousand years. The striking, human-powered paddleboats, now made of fiberglass and other materials, are festooned with incredible colors and intricate carvings of dragon heads. This special place was revitalized by **Riverfront Recapture**, a nonprofit committed to connecting Hartford and East Hartford to the Connecticut River.

See a gorgeous spectacle during the Dragon Boat and Asian Festival at Mortensen Riverfront Plaza. Riverfront Recapture

The Travelers Championship in Cromwell offers great golf along with food trucks and activities.

And don't miss a **Yard Goats** (*www.milb.com/ hartford*) game at **Dunkin' Park**. This minor league baseball team has breathed so much life into Hartford since it debuted in the city in 2017, giving families a relatively inexpensive outing full of fandom and fun. Or head to **Mohegan Sun Casino** (*www .mohegansun.com*) in Uncasville to support the **Connecticut Sun** (*www.sun.wnba.com*), our very own professional team in the WNBA. If you're tired of the heat outside, it's one-stop shopping for a fun day or evening indoors. While there, play the slots or enjoy the shopping and restaurants at this high-end casino, built in 1996. Connecticut is also home to the **Hartford Athletic** (*www.hartfordathletic.com*), a professional soccer team. Visit the city's Dillon Stadium for games taking place June through October. And golf lovers unite! Every June, the **Travelers Championship** (*www.travelers championship.com*), a PGA event at the beautiful TPC River Highlands, brings thousands of spectators to Cromwell.

Hop into a tube and experience quiet stretches and exciting rapids at Farmington River Tubing.

I mentioned the town of New Hartford in the "Winter" section of this book, but it is also home to a popular summer activity: tubing. **Farmington River Tubing** (*www.farmingtonrivertubing.com*) offers families an inexpensive, fun way to get out on the water on a hot day. Just don a life jacket and grab a tube. Head into the bubbling, running water, which includes several sections of mild rapids. The trip downriver differs depending on whether the water is running high or low, but it's a lot of fun in any conditions, a unique mixture of excitement and relaxation.

One of our absolute top family memories revolves around a day when we simply played together in the water and laughed and laughed . . . and laughed some more. This was all thanks

to a very cool outfit, **Lakeside Watersports** (*www .lakesidewatersports.com*), which treats folks to fun on the waters of **Candlewood Lake** (*www.candle woodlakeauthority.org*) in Brookfield. "We teach you how to water-ski, wakeboard, wake-surf, or we just pull you tubing," says owner and head instructor Connor Kostyra. "We also offer a captain's service, where I can drive your own personal boat and give you instruction on watersports or how to use your boat." This is really a great service for those who don't have a boat and don't normally have the opportunity to take the family out for these active excursions.

Go tubing, water-skiing, or wakeboarding on Candlewood Lake with Lakeside Watersports.

"It's great to just be able to go out and not have the hassle of owning one of these boats," says Kostyra, noting how unique this opportunity is for folks. And it's in a sought-after location. "Candlewood Lake has gotten very popular in the past ten years," says Kostyra. "It's kind of the hidden gem of the Northeast." The largest lake in the state has a fascinating history. It was created in the 1920s by Connecticut Light & Power as a place to produce electricity. Today it sports a great relaxed, community vibe. Lakeside Watersports always provides a boat driver and spotter. The boat accommodates groups of ten.

If you've wanted to see an elusive, beautiful, and historically significant landmark off the coast of Guilford, summer could be a time to accomplish this goal. **Faulkner's Island Lighthouse**, built in 1802, is Connecticut's second-oldest lighthouse tower, constructed for a dire reason after numerous accidents and shipwrecks in this rocky area, also an important shipping lane. "The purpose was to guide mariners and light up the darkness to save lives, and that it did," says Joel Helander, Guilford's town historian, also the founder of **Faulkner's Light Brigade** (*www.faulkners lightbrigade.com*), a volunteer effort meant to preserve and maintain this revered landmark. "Long Island Sound was a transportation corridor connecting the two great commercial ports of the Northeast: Boston and New York. Cargos of all kinds would pass through the Sound every single day." The lighthouse, on the National Register of Historic Places, is situated on a crescent-shaped island located 3.5 miles offshore. The brigade aims to provide public access to the island during a once-a-year open house in early

Take a rare opportunity to head out to Faulkner's Island Lighthouse off Guilford's coast, accessible by boat.

September, around Labor Day. "Logistically, it's extremely difficult. This is an offshore island. You can have a bright, sunny day with a scheduled open island event, but the wind is thirty knots and vessels can't go out there safely," says Helander, who also wrote a book about the history of the island. But public outings have happened, sometimes drawing hundreds of people to the island. It remains the only active light station on an island in Connecticut. Some years, folks have even motored or sailed their own boats to the island and anchored them before taking a water taxi to the island. Keep an eye on the brigade's website for information. The island, a breeding colony for an endangered species of tern, is also part of the **Stewart B. McKinney National Wildlife Refuge**.

Connecticut showcases some magnificent foliage during the beautiful autumn months.

Fall

Sure, summer is my favorite season, but autumn in Connecticut is truly a gift. When there's a crispness in the air, we are surrounded by gold and orange hues, vibrant against the blue sky. It's the perfect time to take a brisk walk in one of our state parks or pick a pumpkin in a field full of pure New England charm. Read on to learn all sorts of ways to enjoy this special season to the fullest.

East Haddam: To get to this town's premier destination, simply hop the **Chester-Hadlyme Ferry (portal.ct.gov/DOT/Traveler/ferries/Chester -Hadlyme-Ferry)**, open April through November, for an experience that's both serviceable and enjoyable. The sixty-five-foot ferry, called a "quaint wonder" on the state's website, really saves time. According to the state, traveling from Chester to Lyme via roads, over the East Haddam swing bridge, is a 20.3-mile trip. Taking the ferry knocks that down to 8.3 miles. Besides, it's beautiful. Folks just drive their cars onto the ferry for

Left: Save time and experience history aboard the Chester-Hadlyme Ferry. Right top: Get ready for trick-or-treating; it's fall in Connecticut! Right bottom: See beautiful Chapman Falls at Devil's Hopyard State Park.

An iconic location! Tour the inside and grounds of Gillette Castle, the fanciful home of stage actor William Gillette.

a 15-minute gaze at the lovely Connecticut River. The ferry takes visitors easily to **Gillette Castle State Park (portal.ct.gov/DEEP/State-Parks/ Parks/Gillette-Castle-State-Park)**, a fascinating place that begs to be explored. William Gillette, a stage actor best known for his portrayal of Sherlock Holmes, built a one-of-a kind stone castle between 1913 and 1919. "Twenty stone masons and five carpenters built the home with very modern steam heat, electricity, and running water," says Raymon Knoop, a supervisor at the park. "It cost about a million dollars to build back then. It has twenty-four rooms and is fourteen thousand square feet." Gillette even built railroad tracks around the property, where he would operate a small locomotive, called the Seventh Sister Shortline. "Gillette Castle can provide a family with a guided tour of the castle in season, along with scenic views of the Connecticut River, picnic tables, and hiking trails," says Knoop. The park is open year-round from 8:00 a.m. to sunset. Guided tours of the castle are available seven days a week Memorial Day through Labor Day, then weekends only through Columbus Day. Those with mobility issues are able to enjoy many aspects of the park and castle, such as the visitor center and the goldfish pond. And the downtown area of this lovely town is worth a visit for its fine dining and views of the famous **Goodspeed Opera House (www.goodspeed.org)**, an iconic, white gabled building on the river. Not only striking, the theater treats

Enjoy peace and tranquility, surrounded by animals, at Ray of Light Farm.

the public to fantastic musicals, from world premieres to well-known productions. Another favorite East Haddam spot is **Ray of Light Farm** (**www.rayoflightfarm.org**), an animal sanctuary and therapy center that aims to be a "healing presence," giving folks a reprieve from the stressors of the world. "We offer a place where people can just come and feel good about life," says Bonnie Buongiorne, founder of the nonprofit farm, who ditched her career as a building contractor to pursue this passion after surviving a bout with cancer. "It's been amazing. Every time I have a need, something shows up, so I just live that way." Buongiorne and her helpers rescue and rehabilitate animals. Folks can visit animals such as horses, donkeys, mules, goats, mini-cows, sheep, llamas, pheasants, chickens, geese, ducks, tortoises, and peacocks. While visiting the farm is free, the farm generates income through specialized riding lessons, holidays events, and other unique activities, such as Wellness Walkabouts, which help participants feel good mentally and physically. "We have guinea pig adventures. People come in and sign up to be with guinea pigs for twenty minutes," says Buongiorne. A visit to the farm is a great activity for folks of all abilities. And for outdoor recreation like biking, hiking, fishing, and birding, head to one-thousand-acre **Devil's Hopyard State Park** (**portal.ct.gov/DEEP/State-Parks/Parks/Devils-Hopyard -State-Park**), offering accessibility at the fishing platform and picnic area.

See where the state's most famous war hero taught in 1773.

Don't miss the highlight: beautiful Chapman Falls, with water falling from more than sixty feet. Lastly, drive down a charming driveway, walk past stone pillars up into a beautiful green parcel of land overlooking the Connecticut River, and discover the bright red one-room **Nathan Hale Schoolhouse (www.sarconnecticut.org/historic-sites/nathan-hale -schoolhouse-east-haddam/)**, a re-creation of where the state's most famous war hero taught in 1773. The lovely schoolhouse, owned and operated by the Sons of the American Revolution, with wooden benches and a brick fireplace, is flanked by a Charter Oak, Connecticut's State Tree. Nearby is a monument to Major General Joseph Spencer, a local soldier and statesman. Tours, featuring delightful docents, run weekends through the end of September. Grounds are level and doable for those with mobility issues.

Old Lyme: On a gorgeous September evening, board the Riverquest (**www.ctriverquest.com**), docked at the **Connecticut River Museum** (**www.ctrivermuseum.org**) in Essex, for an incredibly beloved, unique event, the **Swallow Spectacular**. "It's a unique, on-the-water experience," says Cathy Malin, director of visitor experience for the museum. The boat heads downriver to a particular spot in Old Lyme where these birds like to sleep for the night. But their process of heading to rest is both visual and fascinating. "They come every evening just after sunset and do this amazing ballet in the sky," says Malin, describing the dark cloud they make, moving overhead. That's when the depth of the action becomes apparent. Layer upon layer of birds are flying around yet staying within the confines of the cloud's perimeter, creating a one-of-a-kind image that looks something like fireworks or shooting stars. Typically, the swallows converge at dusk and can come from as far as

Riverquest takes visitors out to see the incredible Swallow Spectacular on the banks of the Connecticut River.

twenty-five miles away. The swallows' nightly ritual lasts for about a half hour, then they go down into the reeds to sleep for the night. "It's different every night. The numbers are astounding. There are upwards of a half million birds in the sky at once," says Malin. *Riverquest* (also described in the "Winter" section of this book) is an ecotour vessel that can accommodate wheelchairs and walkers. Folks can bring along a picnic dinner with drinks. The museum's other boat, *OnRust*, a re-creation of explorer Adrian Block's boat, built in 1614, also takes the public on tours to see the swallows, but it is not accessible due to its historic nature. Old Lyme boasts another incredibly special place: the **Florence Griswold Museum (www.florencegriswoldmuseum.org)**. "Our museum celebrates art, history, and nature. Our history is of the Lyme Art Colony, where artists came to paint at Miss Florence's Boarding House which is on the site," says Tammi Flynn, director of marketing, noting that the colony was known for American Impressionism. In addition to her home, a late Georgian mansion, find a modern art space, the Krieble Gallery, celebrating Griswold's passion for art and showcasing around three exhibits a year. The experience doesn't end there. Using the gorgeous grounds on the banks of the Lieutenant River as a space for creativity has been the norm since Miss Florence's students set up their easels here years ago. And in the fall the expansive yard, part of the Robert F. Schumann Artists' Trail, is filled with magic. It's the Wee Faerie

The Wee Faerie Village at the Florence Griswold Museum has delighted more than 175,000 guests.
Florence Griswold Museum

Village, which since 2009 has delighted more than 175,000 guests. "People make a pilgrimage to it," says Flynn. "It's really a way to get people to do something fun and different and family oriented in October." More than two dozen whimsical houses are created by local artists and nestled into the landscape outside the museum. Visitors go house to house, enjoying intricate details that delight the imagination. I took the boys for several years, and we always had so much fun. It's truly an enjoyable afternoon for everyone from toddlers to senior citizens. The first floor of the historic home, the education center, and the gallery are fully accessible. Special pathways make much of the grounds accessible as well. The museum is part of the Old Lyme Arts District, which also includes the **Lyme Academy of Fine Arts (www.lymeacademy.edu)** and the **Lyme Art Association (www.lymeartassociation.org)**. This beautiful town on Long Island Sound sports some gorgeous beaches but many of them are private in the summer. The offseason, especially fall, is a great time to throw a Frisbee or stroll around **White Sands Beach**, which leads to The Nature Conservancy's Griswold Point Preserve. **Sound View Beach (www.soundviewbeach.org)**, dating back to the late 1800s, is considered America's first public beach. **Blackhall Outfitters (www.blackhall outfitters.com)**, with a companion store located in Westbrook (and detailed in that town's section of this book), provides folks the opportunity to rent kayaks or paddleboards for a few hours or the day to experience the beauty of the Great Island Wildlife Area. "Anyone can come; you don't need paddling experience. There's some tutorial on the dock," says owner Gene Chmiel, who believes this is a simple, turnkey way to enjoy the water. "Two hours is forty bucks. We think this is an affordable activity for a couple, a family, a mom looking to get her kids outside." The store and rental center also offer guided sunset paddle tours at beautiful Griswold Point, where participants can watch the sunset over a lighthouse in Old Saybrook.

Simsbury: Fall is a great time of year to take a hike to the **Heublein Tower (portal.ct.gov/DEEP/State-Parks/Parks/Talcott-Mountain-State -Park)**, affording one of the best views in all of Connecticut. Absorb the beauty of the foliage during a hike on one of three paths through Talcott Mountain State Park, located on the border of Bloomfield and Simsbury, one of the few state parks open year-round. The first part of the 1.25-mile path is steep but graduates into a terrain that's wide and flat. One-third of the way up, the trees open and the first fabulous glimpse of the valley below comes into view as the Farmington River winds through the landscape. On a crystal-clear day, five states are visible from this spot.

After about forty-five minutes along the trail, the destination is clear. "Gilbert Heublein was up there with his then fiancée and said, 'Someday I'm going to build you a tower here on this mountain,' and in 1911 he had acquired enough land to do that," says Jay Willerup, president of the board of directors of the Friends of Heublein Tower, a volunteer group that helps run the operation. The tower, considered an early skyscraper with a Bavarian influence, was designed by the same architects who worked on the governor's residence in Hartford. Finished in 1914, it

Folks can hike up to the iconic Heublein Tower, with sweeping views of the Farmington River.

became the summer home of Heublein, a hotelier and restaurateur. The state purchased Talcott Mountain in 1966, transforming the entire area into a state park, which opened in 1974. Take 110 steps to the top of the tower with an incredible panoramic view from 1,000 feet above the river. "It's so unique. On a clear day you can see to the New York border, up into Massachusetts, and all the way down to Sleeping Giant," says Willerup, noting that an astounding quarter of a million people visit the park each year. The tower is open Friday, Saturday, Sunday, and Monday. This outing is free. Unfortunately, the tower is only accessed by walking trails, and the old-fashioned tower stairs are difficult to navigate for those with mobility issues. However, it is easy to traverse the path over the beautifully unique **Old Drake Hill Flower Bridge** (**www.simsbury-ct.gov/culture-parks -recreation/pages/the-old-drake-hill-flower-bridge**), a metal truss bridge from the late 1800s. The 183-foot-long bridge stretches over the Farmington River and is festooned with blooms, thanks to numerous flower boxes that line the bridge. The bridge, appropriate for biking and walking, is on the National Register of Historic Places. Through the fall, enjoy a tasting at **Rosedale Farms & Vineyards** (**www.rosedale1920 .com**), known for its handcrafted wines, both sweet and dry. Both **Massacoe State Forest** (**portal.ct.gov/DEEP/State-Parks/Forests/ Massacoe-State-Forest**) and **Stratton Brook State Park** (**portal.ct.gov/ DEEP/State-Parks/Parks/Stratton-Brook-State-Park**) offer great hiking, biking, and birding.

Take a lovely stroll over the Old Drake Hill Flower Bridge, festooned with blooms in season.

Newtown: It's exploring with a twist! Welcome to the wild, woolly world of llama hiking. "I enjoy bringing people together with animals and getting them out in nature in a different way," says A. J. Collier, who owns the only licensed llama hiking company in the state, based at **Rowanwood Farm** (**www.rowanwoodfarm.com**). "It's a calming,

Make a furry friend during a llama hike, courtesy of Rowanwood Farm.

peaceful way to be outdoors. It's also a fun way to spend time with friends." After an introduction, Bolivian, Chilean, Peruvian, and Argentinean mini-llamas lead folks on a one-hour hike through the forest, accompanied by experienced guides. Activity level is easy to moderate. Llamas are slow walkers, but when they see a stream, they take a dip! Why stroll with a llama, you ask? Because it's fun! Llamas are like your family dog, but a little different too. "Llamas are domesticated. They don't exist in the wild. They're raised as a pet, so they do respond very well to their caretakers. But when they meet new people, it's kind of like 'stranger danger' where they don't know you. It takes them a while to trust you," says Collier. But during the hikes, they do warm up, and once you're good friends, they may even offer you a llama kiss! These animals really crave exercise, so they love this walk through the woods. This adventure is for adults and children, age eight and up. Collier says the hikes require a participant to be mobile, but for folks that need it, she can customize some time with the llamas. "The people who want to experience llamas that maybe can't do a physical hike, I suggest they come to the farm for a fun tour and meet all the llamas here," she says. Newtown, full of charm, is the fifth-largest town in the state. So there is a lot of room to play out in nature at **Paugussett State Forest (portal .ct.gov/DEEP/State-Parks/Locate-Park-Forest/Other-State-Parks-and -Forests#Paugusssett)**. Take part in hiking, biking, and letterboxing. There's a gorgeous thirty-foot waterfall at **Rocky Glen State Park (portal .ct.gov/DEEP/State-Parks/Locate-Park-Forest/Other-State-Parks-and -Forests#RockyGlen)** along with forty-six acres, including hiking trails. The kids will love a stop at **EverWonder Children's Museum (www .everwondermuseum.org)**, inspiring curiosity and learning in young children. See little creatures like frogs, fish, and a snake. Dig for dinosaur fossils in a sandpit. Explore the technology corner, complete with an iPad lab. And get an intro course in engineering, thanks to a car racing ramp and a Lego table. And now to a destination for the adults: **Aquila's Nest Vineyards (www.aquilasnestvineyards.com)**, a four-thousand-square-foot facility perched on a hilltop offering all kinds of wines. This location is pet-friendly and ADA compliant.

East Hampton: In the fall, **Paul and Sandy's Too (www.paulsand sandys.com)**, a garden center and hardware store, transforms into **Pumpkintown USA (www.pumpkintown.com)**. And the story behind this destination is fascinating. "Fall is generally a slow time for our industry. During a day trip to Vermont, thirty-plus years ago, owners Paul

See a variety of pumpkin people living in Pumpkintown at Paul and Sandy's Too! Paul and Sandy's Too

and Sandy Peszynski stumbled across a display of life-size scarecrows with pumpkin heads that many people were stopping to look at. On the drive back home, Paul decided he could build some and display them in front of the business," says Karen Clark, one of the business partners. "The display became a popular attraction that fall, and plans for a town and more characters were born." We used to go every year and always enjoyed this fun autumnal day trip. Folks walk through the town to see pumpkin people in various

Appreciate nature at Shipyard Falls, a waterfall on Mine Brook.

scenes: at the firehouse, church, saloon, post office, and bank. Over the years, creators added "The Ride," an opportunity for families to drive through a larger village scene in the woods in the comfort of their own car. "Both Pumpkintown Village and The Ride at Pumpkintown provide families with a fun, non-scary fall adventure with many interactive activities for kids and photo opportunities," says Clark. Get cider and doughnuts, and enjoy this autumnal treat!! Pumpkintown is accessible for wheelchairs and strollers. Also be sure to check out one of the last covered bridges in the state, located in East Hampton. The **Comstock Covered Bridge** crosses over the Salmon River. This ADA-compliant site is for people only, no vehicles. Stop by **Shipyard Falls**, a waterfall on Mine Brook that folks can view from a small bridge on Shipyard Road, a tight, residential area. Beware, though: There's a small spot on the side of the street where folks can pull over, but there is no defined parking for this location. A path from the road leads visitors down to the brook for a better view. Find more great scenery and exercise opportunities at **Hurd State Park** (**portal.ct.gov/DEEP/State-Parks/ Parks/Hurd-State-Park**). We

Take the dogs for a stroll or fish in the Connecticut River at Hurd State Park.

brought the dogs for a journey along the River Trail, which leads down to sandy beaches on the Connecticut River where kids were playing and folks were fishing. The well-defined trail winds through some interesting glacial landscape with hills and ledges. Lastly, don't miss a chance to support **Connecticut Draft Horse Rescue (www.ctdraftrescue.org)**, located at Autumn Ridge, a twenty-acre farm for rescued horses like Clydesdales, who are rehabilitated and even re-homed. This wonderful organization hosts multiple family events every year.

Meriden: Head to beautiful **Hubbard Park (www.meridenct.gov/ city-services/parks-and-recreation/hubbard-park/)**, a natural oasis in this busy city. Justin Piccirillo, a teacher and author from Meriden, has written a book about the park, which has a fascinating history. American industrialist Walter Hubbard became burned out from his business ventures, so he turned his attention to nature. "All the money he stockpiled went into clearing land around what they called the Hanging Hills. Lo and behold, he created a park," explains Piccirillo, adding that Hubbard donated the park to the city in 1900, creating fun for generations to come. "It offers so much. It has tennis courts, a pool, and a children's playground. No matter your age, there's something for everyone there." Beautiful Mirror Lake is the park's centerpiece. While there's a popular daffodil festival in the spring and a massive light

Hubbard Park is a natural oasis in the busy city of Meriden. Lynne Vigue

display during the holiday season, in fall the park is known for some great leaf peeping opportunities. "People like to call it the crown jewel of Meriden," says Kathy Matula, recreation coordinator for the city, who leads hikes around the park each month year-round, some to promote good mental health. "People come to visit from all over the world. On a clear day you can see all the way to Long Island Sound. You can see Sleeping Giant." Head to Castle Craig, a stone observation tower atop the park, offering incredible views of Connecticut. Between May and October, you can drive to the castle, 1,002 feet above sea level. While people often hike or bike to the castle, Matula says that senior citizens and those with mobility issues find the drive to be very convenient. The park offers many accessible spots. Find great hiking trails and picnic spots all throughout the park. Volunteers recently updated the signage, and on the trails, every marker shaped like a castle leads folks to Castle Craig. "It's a park for all," says Matula, who believes it's the perfect spot for getting exercise or soaking up the pages of a good book. The park is on the National Register of Historic Places. Also check out beautiful **Giuffrida Park** (**www .meridenlandtrust.org**), with hiking trails to Chauncey Peak and Mount Lamentation, featuring a scenic ridge walk with incredible views. The fifty-mile Mattabesett Trail also cuts through that mountain.

New Haven: The Elm City is a beautiful, bustling place filled with stunning architecture and cultural interest. Much of the activity revolves around the ivy-covered Gothic buildings of Yale University. Recently I went on a field trip with my son to the **Yale University Art Gallery (www.artgallery.yale .edu)** and could not have been more impressed. This is a bright, airy emporium of fine art that, in my opinion, could rival any art museum around the globe. Built in 1832, this incredible space is the oldest university art museum in the country, containing more than three hundred thousand

The Yale Art Gallery, on the campus of the prestigious university, contains incredible masterpieces.

Left: The Yale Art Gallery features works by Claude Monet and Vincent van Gogh. Right: Stroll through the largest collection of British art outside the United Kingdom.

objects, from African to ancient to modern art. The museum consists of two conjoined buildings. One, featuring arches, cornices, and big windows, was completed in 1928. The other is more modern, finished in 1953 and renovated in the late 1990s. I was completely wowed by pieces like *The Night Café* by Vincent van Gogh and *The Artist's Garden at Giverny* by Claude Monet. Outfitted with ramps and elevators, the gallery is accessible to those with disabilities. Across the street, find the **Yale Center for British Art** (**www.britishart.yale.edu**), another incredibly impressive stroll through the largest collection of British art outside the United Kingdom. See portraits of aristocracy, along with photographs and rare books. Walking through the Long Gallery, a rectangular room filled with paintings from floor to ceiling, feels like strolling through a scene from *Harry Potter*. The galleries are accessible by wheelchair. And we can't forget the **Yale Peabody Museum** (**www.peabody.yale.edu**), a spot my boys loved when they were young. Why, you ask? Dinosaur bones! Recently reopened after a major renovation, this accessible museum contains more than fourteen million specimens and objects telling the story of Earth's history and cultures. For book lovers, a stop at the **Beinecke Rare Book & Manuscript Library** (**www.beinecke.library .yale.edu**), on Yale's campus, is an absolute must, if only for the sheer visual impact. Walk into the stunning accessible building and see a six-story tower containing 180,000 books. Some are incredibly meaningful books, such as an early edition of J. M. Barrie's *Peter Pan*. What's New Haven without pizza? Colin Caplan founded **Taste of New Haven** (**www .tasteofnewhaven.com**) in 2011, offering general food tours around the city, but the tours involving 'za certainly took off! "Our pizza tours are walking tours. They last four to six hours, and we usually hit four pizza spots. We eat anywhere from twelve to fifteen slices—sampling, discussing, learning about the history of pizza, Italian immigration, New Haven, and neighborhoods. And in the end, everyone is one big happy pizza family," he laughs. Then came the **Elm City Party Bike** (**www .elmcitypartybike.com**), a rolling celebration through the city. Eight to fifteen people can fit on this big bike, outfitted with refreshments, which offers a two-hour look at the sites and architecture. "Connecticut people are always looking for a great time; we just happened to find a new, novel, fun thing, and people literally climbed on and started pedaling," he says. "It's that feeling of being a child again, pedaling and being in a social environment. It's a little bit of a gathering, a party, just being on the town and being seen. It's that feeling of exploration, finding something new."

The Elm City Party Bike is a rolling celebration through the city. Elm City Party Bike

Berlin: This busy town, filled with minigolf and batting cages aplenty, offers a good school system and one beloved event, the **Berlin Fair** (**www.ctberlinfair.com**), dating back to 1882. It's held every year the weekend after Labor Day, when organizers are often blessed with great weather and stellar attendance. "We try to give folks the best experience

Kids get a day off from school for a beloved tradition, the Berlin Fair. Berlin Fair

possible at a fair," says Lenny Tubbs, assistant entertainment superintendent and the marketing and advertising superintendent for the Berlin Lions Club, which puts on the fair. "Our fairgrounds are second to none in Connecticut. Most areas are accessible, because we have paved roads going through it." The fair is the club's major fundraiser and draws up to seventy thousand visitors. The club donates thousands of dollars back into community programs for youths, sports teams, Girl and Boy Scouts troops, and more. The fair is a cherished, memorable time for so many families. "There's a tradition in Berlin. We close our schools Friday morning," says Tubbs, noting that this day off from school encourages families to take part. Kids under age eleven can attend the fair for free. "We've got amusement rides and carnival games," says Tubbs, proud that the fair isn't full of out-of-town food trucks. "The majority of our food is from local groups." Find animal acts, craft shows, musical concerts, and much more. Berlin is also home to **Lamentation Mountain State Park** (**portal.ct.gov/DEEP/State-Parks/Locate-Park-Forest/Other-State-Parks -and-Forests#LamentationMountainand**), forty-seven acres of natural beauty with hiking trails and lovely views. **Ragged Mountain Memorial Preserve (www.berlinct.gov/egov/documents/270bfb06_dca1_4918 _3a1b_ada3b9d356fb.pdf**) offers a lovely walking path. In the Kensington section of town, the adventurous find **CT Ballooning** (**www.ctballooning.com**), offering hot air balloon rides in the morning, just after sunrise. "We get bucket list requests, birthdays, anniversaries, proposals; we even do weddings in the balloon. I'm an ordained minister," says owner James Regan. "We go anywhere from just above the treetops to a couple thousand feet in altitude. We travel anywhere from three to ten miles during the flight, so we get a nice variety of views.

Embark on an incredible trip with CT Ballooning, operating out of Kensington. Mathew Dutkiewicz

Where we fly here in central Connecticut, we see Long Island Sound, Sleeping Giant, Hartford, and all the way to Mount Holyoke. On clear days you can see Mount Greylock up in Massachusetts. The Litchfield Hills are visible." He says that most of the time, folks aren't scared. The trip feels stable in the basket. While the whole experience takes about three and a half hours, visitors are in the air for one hour. The experience ends with an on-ground champagne toast.

Lebanon: Drive down the bucolic streets of this quintessentially New England town and see classic farms and green fields. It's not only charming but also filled with historical significance thanks to its prominent role in the Revolutionary War. In fact, it's known as the "Heartbeat of the Revolution." Here, find the **War Office (www .sarconnecticut.org/historic-sites/trumbull-war-office/)**, owned and run by the Sons of the American Revolution. "It's where Governor Jonathan Trumbull turned his store into a supply house for items for people serving in the Revolutionary War," says property steward David Packard, explaining that this is also where Trumbull met with dignitaries

Left: Governor Jonathan Trumbull turned his store into a supply house during the Revolutionary War. Right: The Governor Trumbull House is owned and operated by the Daughters of the American Revolution.

such as George Washington. French officials, the Marquis de Lafayette, and Comte de Rochambeau spent part of 1781 in Lebanon before heading to Yorktown, Virginia. The museum is composed of two rooms: Trumbull's office and a meeting room, where supplies were stored. "There are barrels, bags of grain, sugar, clothing, blankets, drums, fifes, canteens," says Packard, noting that the museum has two authentic items on display. "We have a Revolutionary War sword that was donated to us, and we have an original musket." The museum is open June through September. Knowledgeable docents greet visitors and share valuable information. Due to the historic nature of the building, the War Office is not wheelchair accessible. Learn more about this era at the **Governor Trumbull House (www.govtrumbullhousedar.org)**, owned and operated by the Daughters of the American Revolution, open the second Saturday of each month. The house is listed on the National Register of Historic Places. The house is not wheelchair accessible due to its age. Next door, folks can see the **Wadsworth Stable**, which is accessible and home to a fascinating story. Originally in Hartford, it housed George Washington's horses in 1780. When the building was threatened with demolition in 1950, philanthropist Katherine Seymour Day (mentioned in the "Hartford" section of this book) raised money to have it moved and rebuilt in Lebanon. Now visitors can see farm tools and antique wagons there. Folks can also see the **Jonathan Trumbull Jr. House (www .lebanonct.gov/jonathan-trumbull-jr-house)**, which belonged to the governor's son, also a politician, who worked in the war effort. Trumbull Jr. served as George Washington's military secretary and eventually became governor himself. This house, built around 1769, is located in the Lebanon Green National Register District and is ADA compliant. It's

Left: In its original location, the Wadsworth Stable once housed George Washington's horses. Right: See the home of Jonathan Trumbull Jr., a politician who worked in the Revolutionary War effort.

beautiful. The green is different from most—large and filled with wild grasses and flowers. Locals and visitors alike can enjoy a walking path through this scenic area. For a look at Trumbull Jr.'s lovely home, contact the **Lebanon Historical Society** (**www.historyoflebanon.org**).

Wilton: My father, a well-read and always interesting man, told me about **Weir Farm National Historical Park** (**www.nps.gov/wefa/index .htm**) years ago. He said, "Sarah, it's the only national park dedicated to Impressionist painting. It sounds really special." And, boy, was he right. It took me all these years to get there, but thanks to writing this book,

I scheduled a visit and had such an enjoyable morning at this beautiful property. The farm was the summer home of J. Alden Weir, considered a pioneer in American Impressionism. Known as "Julian" to family and friends, he lived here from 1882 to 1919. He invited contemporaries to paint *en plein air* (in plain air)

Weir Farm, including J. Alden Weir's summer home, is the only national park dedicated to Impressionist painting.

in what he believed was "the perfect setting": the fields of this incredible sixty-eight-acre property where there's so much to explore. It was designated as a national park in 1990 after a fifteen-year grassroots effort by local citizens, museum curators, and art enthusiasts. Tremendous effort was put into keeping the grounds authentic for visitors. "They're seeing the park as it would have looked when Weir was here," says Park Superintendent Linda Cook. Park rangers give tours of the first floor

See the historic studio where Weir created his works of art.

of the farmhouse, which bears the words "Here shall we rest and call content our home" outside the front door. Inside, see several originals of Weir's work, such as *Early Moonrise*. Weir loved to paint in the early morning or evening. Most fascinating to me were the two historic art studios next to the home. The Weir Studio, restored to represent the year 1915, when he would have been creating masterpieces in the rustic space, is filled with brushes, paints, and palettes. The nearby Young Studio belonged to sculptor Mahonri Mackintosh Young, who married Weir's daughter, Dorothy; both were artists who also worked at the farm.

The well-established Pond Trail at Weir Farm is part of the property's "artscape."

It's a stunning open space with abundant light and a loft containing books and items of interest. But a visit to the farm isn't complete without outside exploration, which includes "walking the artscape" with a comprehensive brochure. "There are about 250 known painting sites. Some of them are mapped and strategically shared with visitors so they can navigate the landscape and stand where a painting was made and created and today see that same landscape," says Cook, using a work titled *The Laundry*, which now resides at the Wadsworth Atheneum in Hartford, as an example. "You can see where that painting site is and match it to the painting and really appreciate the vantage point of the artist, the light that happened that day, the season." This experience enhances a visitor's connection to art. The artscape takes folks through sublime gardens, which include a storybook Secret Garden, manicured in a relaxed New England

Visitors are invited to touch a reproduction of Weir's work Ella and Lady Lee *to learn about the art of Impressionism.*

way, with beautiful flowers surrounded by rustic stone walls. Continue this experience during a two-mile round-trip walk to Weir Pond on a well-established trail. Along the way, visitors see a small portable studio where Weir would keep art supplies near the woods. Around the pond, find families fishing and dogs running around the trails. I finished up my trip to the farm with time in the thoughtful visitor center. Folks can view more art and are even invited to "touch a painting" to learn about the art of Impressionism. The reproduction of Weir's work *Ella and Lady Lee* shows the texture of the style, which involved layers of thick paint and visible brush strokes. Outside the center, find backpacks filled with art supplies that visitors are encouraged to borrow so they can create their own masterpieces in these storied fields. "We have well over two thousand painters and artists who paint here every year. They love to come here. They know they're welcome here. They feel like they belong and we want them to be out there," says Cook. Truly, a visit to this destination is peaceful, refreshing, and fascinating. The grounds are open year-round. The visitor center, farmhouse, and studios are open May through October. The house and one room of the visitor center are wheelchair accessible, and there are accessible paths on the grounds. The studios are not accessible, but Weir Farm offers virtual tours. For more outdoor recreation, head to the **Wilton Town Forest (www.wiltonct.org/ conservation-commission/pages/trail-maps)**, with a waterfall called Sheep Falls. The **Belknap Preserve** includes lush fields and sturdy stone walls that show off the town's agricultural past.

Avon: This lovely town, once named the third-safest town in the country by *Money* magazine, has great schools, including a well-known boarding school for boys, **Avon Old Farms (www.avonoldfarms.com)**. It's also home to the **First Company Governor's Horse Guard (portal.ct.gov/ MIL/Organization/Governors-Guards/1GHG/1GHG-Home-Page)**, founded in 1778 as one of the four organized militia units in the state. This unit engages in crowd control during big events and even helps during emergencies. It's considered the oldest continuously active cavalry unit in the country. The public can see drills on Thursday evenings. Kids can participate in Our Little Heroes, a monthly program aimed to teach about the safety and maintenance of horses. On-site, gaze upon the **Horse Guards Barn**, built in 1880; not currently in use, it's on the

The public can see the First Company Governor's Horse Guard drills each week.

State Register of Historic Places. Nearby is the 105-acre **Horse Guard State Park** (**portal.ct.gov/DEEP/State-Parks/Locate-Park-Forest/ Other-State-Parks-and-Forests#HorseGuard**), which offers great views, especially during foliage season. For advice about great hikes, check out the website **Explore CT** (**www.explorect.org**), which says this "scenic reserve" offers a fairly easy 1.2-mile walk to a lovely overlook where folks can gaze out upon the northwest hills. The last part of the hike, however, involves scaling some rocks. Check out the **Pine Grove Schoolhouse**, in use from 1865 to 1949. This location, open Sundays through September, shows visitors small, classic desks, a water pump, and brass bells used by the teachers. View a similar scene at another one-room schoolhouse, **Schoolhouse No. 3**, both maintained by the Historical Society. Let's close out this town with a particularly unique and beloved location: **BeanZ & Co.** (**www.beanzandco.com**)—more than a café, often considered a destination. Five years ago, moms Kim Morrison and Noelle Alix were inspired by their daughters, Megan and Kate, who both have Down syndrome. "They were aging out of the school system, and we wanted to figure out a way to literally just give the two of them jobs," says Morrison. So they revitalized Morrison's café and turned it into a place that provides work for those of all abilities. Today they have provided employment not just for their daughters but for dozens of other young adults as well. The employees are paid and work alongside typical peers, who provide training. The BeanZ crew, often wearing shirts with the slogan "Everyone Belongs," recently moved into a new five-thousand-square-foot location, meant to be a gathering place for everyone, including those with special needs. "It turned into something much bigger than we ever thought it would be," says Morrison, grateful for the community support. "We think we've created a place where they have a purposeful day and meaningful employment." It goes without saying, this location is accessible for all visitors.

Thomaston: Known as "A Town for All Time," Thomaston is home to two beloved Connecticut destinations. See the gorgeous foliage from a vintage train! The whole family will enjoy a visit to the **Railroad Museum of New England** (**www.rmne.org**), which offers an Autumn Limited Colors Ride on the Naugatuck Railroad. Passengers will delight in the gorgeous views of the Litchfield Hills, the Naugatuck River, and the Thomaston Dam. But wait, there's an added perk. "We stop at **Fascia's Chocolates** (**www.faschoc.com**) in Waterbury on those trains. So on top of getting

The Railroad Museum of New England offers the Autumn Limited Colors Ride and the Pumpkin Patch Train. Railroad Museum of New England

unique views of the river and the railroad that you can't see from your car, you also get to stop at the chocolate factory and check that out," says Orion Newall, passenger operations director for the Naugatuck Railroad. This destination is run by an organization committed to sharing the region's rich history along the rails. "You start your journey at a station from 1881, and you're riding in our oldest in-service passenger car. This year it turns one hundred," says Newall. Kids also love to experience the super-popular Pumpkin Patch Train, where they can take a ride, pick a pumpkin, and enjoy the fun. Apple cider is served during the trip. Both of these excursions last one hour and twenty minutes. Fascia's Chocolates also collaborates for fall festivals at the Thomaston station, where folks can enjoy cornhole and hay bale tossing. Throughout the year, there are special train rides for Easter, Christmas, and other occasions. Each year, the railroad collaborates with an autism support group called Sun, Moon & Stars to provide sensory-friendly experiences for those on the spectrum. For those with mobility challenges, a wheelchair lift can assist folks onto the historic train. Also, don't miss a stop at the **Thomaston Opera House**, operated by the **Landmark Community Theater** (**www .landmarkcommunitytheatre.org**). The opera house occupies floors two and three above the town hall, which was part of the original design in 1883. "When this building was built, the town fathers wanted to create a downtown and a centerpiece for the town," says Jeffrey Dunn, executive director for Landmark Community Theater and chairman of the town's Economic Development Commission, noting the iconic clock tower atop the building, which is listed on the National Register of Historic Places. "We have a 1926 Marr & Colton theater pipe organ that plays before most of our performances." The theater puts on eighty shows a year, including plays, concerts, and even a children's theater series. The opera house has an elevator, making it accessible. Even more provisions are in the works. "We're working now to create more access to the stage so that people with mobility issues are able to perform," says Dunn. He says Thomaston is on the rise, with more than twenty restaurants in town where folks can dine before a performance.

Enfield: Right on the border with Massachusetts, this agricultural town is filled with green space and history. Take the kids to the one-room **Wallop School**, which served students from 1800 to the 1940s, for a lesson in simplicity. "They learn about the difference in the school year from now to then. Then, boys went to school a different number of days than girls because the boys had to leave early in the spring to plant; they started school late in the fall after harvesting," explains Michael Miller, secretary of the **Enfield Historical Society (www.enfieldhistoricalsociety.org)**,

See the one-room Wallop School, which served students from 1800 through the 1940s.

See the home of Martha Parsons, a trailblazer honored in the Connecticut Women's Hall of Fame.

which oversees the school. "They get to see what it was like when you didn't have the internet or any technology beyond your pen, pencil, or slate. We have all the different incarnations of the tools that were used by the kids." The school is wheelchair accessible with assistance. The society also manages the **Martha A. Parsons House**, honoring a woman who is in the **Connecticut Women's Hall of Fame** (**www.cwhf.org**). "She was the executive secretary, one of the officers of Landers, Frary and Clark in New Britain in the early 1900s," says Miller of Parsons's role at a housewares company. "She was an executive when women weren't really executives. In fact, she had to sign all of her paperwork 'M. A. Parsons' so the other businesses they were working with didn't know they were communicating with a woman." Due to the historic nature of the building, it is not wheelchair accessible. Also head to the **Old Town Hall Museum**, wheelchair accessible on the first floor, to learn about the Shaker community that lived in Enfield until 1917, along with other local history. "We talk about the carpet industry in Thompsonville and the Hazard Powder company in Hazardville, which made gunpowder," says Miller. These museums, open to the public free of charge, have some regular hours spring through fall and are always open by appointment. Fall is the perfect time to visit **Easy Pickin's Orchard** (**www.easy pickinsorchard.com**) to get pumpkins, gourds, and apples. Folks can also

take a wagon ride. Lastly, take a hike at **Scantic River State Park** (**portal
.ct.gov/-/media/DEEP/stateparks/maps/ScanticRiverWestpdf.pdf**),
particularly beautiful when bathed in the golden colors of fall.

Torrington: This city in the Litchfield Hills is rich with history and has
a promising future thanks to recent revitalization. One of Torrington's
jewels is the **Warner Theatre** (**www.warnertheatre.org**). "The
Warner Theater was built in 1931 by the Warner Brothers," explains
Relationship Director Lesley Budny of the famous cinematic company.
"Our main theater was built as a movie palace to premiere Warner
films. We were one of four hundred such venues across the United
States, and we're one of four left in existence." Budny can't believe the
beauty and history that's been lost and is grateful residents saved the
Warner when it was threatened with demolition in the 1980s. "After a
seventeen-million-dollar capital campaign, there was a full restoration of
our main theater, so it's exactly the quality it was back in 1931. You will
not be disappointed when you walk through the doors. It is absolutely
spectacular and majestic," she says. The theater now offers a plethora
of performances to audiences. "We have around twenty-four national

The Warner Theatre was built in 1931 by the Warner Brothers. The Warner Theatre

touring acts that come through our theater annually, including rock and roll stars, musicians of every type, and comedians," she explains. "On top of that, we have a regional community theater effort where we have five productions annually, four in our studio theater; a three-hundred-seat black box venue; and one big production in our main theater, which has seventeen hundred seats." Find accessible seating and sensory-friendly offerings for children on the autism spectrum. The theater also offers behind-the-scenes tours, which include a look at an eight-thousand-square-foot costume shop, one of only a few in Connecticut that rents out items nationwide. Budny says Torrington has experienced a rebirth in the last decade. "We have formed the second-only cultural historic district in Connecticut," she says, noting that art galleries, **the historical society (www.torringtonhistoricalsociety.org)**, and the library are all involved. "It's one-stop shopping. If you're looking for the arts or a gallery experience or looking to see a show and have a robust dining experience, it's all right here within three blocks." She points out a new popular hot spot called **Bad Dog Brewery (www.bdbrewco.com)**, not far from the theater. Also, be sure to bring the little ones to **KidsPlay Children's Museum (www.kidsplaymuseum.org)**, dedicated to helping children learn and explore in a hands-on, creative way. Even though Torrington is a city, it boasts several incredible parks, dedicated to outdoor recreation. **Burr Pond State Park (portal.ct.gov/DEEP/State-Parks/Parks/Burr -Pond-State-Park)** was the location of the first condensed milk factory, in 1857, which was valuable to soldiers during the Civil War. The mill eventually burned in a fire. It's now an ideal spot for fishing and picnicking. No alcohol is permitted in the park, and parking is limited. Folks can also hike out to gorgeous **Burr Falls** on the eastern side of the park. The park is ADA compliant.

Easton: When you're in this beautiful rural town, make a stop at **Silverman's Farm (www.silvermansfarm.com)**; you won't be sorry. It's a delightful place with so much to offer. During the fall, find pick-your-own pumpkins and apples—but wait, the fun doesn't stop there. "We have a market with all kinds of fresh produce, gifts, flowers, and more. We have a great animal farm with over one hundred animals," says owner Irv Silverman. "We have everything from buffalo to baby pigs; also goats, sheep, llamas, deer, alpacas, emus, donkeys, and Scotch Highland cattle." Visitors are literally waiting at the ticket window before the 9:00 a.m. opening on weekends, eager to take their kids to this well-maintained

See animals, pick berries, and shop for seasonal treats at Silverman's Farm.

attraction with covered picnic tables and plenty of places to sit in the shade and relax. Families can buy a bag of feed so that kids can give food to the animals themselves. They can also enjoy a play area with small tractors and trains that kids can climb on for play. Children also adore a trip in the Orchard Express, with a locomotive in the front and cars that resemble wagons in the back. This fun vehicle takes visitors up into the fields, set on a scenic slope in this country town. Before you leave, don't forget to pick up a jug of fresh-pressed apple cider! This location is ADA compliant. Find plenty of hiking opportunities at **Trout Brook Valley State Park Reserve (portal.ct.gov/DEEP/State-Parks/Locate-Park -Forest/Other-State-Parks-and-Forests#TroutBrookValley)**, a beautiful three-hundred-acre spot where folks can find peace and reflection. Please note: Dogs are not allowed at this reserve.

Woodbury: This historic town, set in the beautiful Litchfield Hills, is known as the "Antiques Capital of Connecticut," with about thirty shops. Turns out, poking around for a treasure is a big tourism draw. "We have independent dealers that have specialties of their own, so we have 'experts in the field' of French and English antiques, early American antiques, folk art, and some mid-century modern," says Karen Reddington-Hughes, president of the **Woodbury Antiques Dealers Association. (www.antiqueswoodbury.com)**. "The people you will

Woodbury is known as the "Antiques Capital of Connecticut," with about thirty shops.

see are people who are very renowned in their fields of antiques; many of them, early on, were on *Antiques Roadshow*. Some of them specialized in weather vanes, clocks, rugs, all different types of items." These stores are also part of the state's **Antiques Trail (www.ctvisit.com/antiques trail).**"It gives somebody, if they're a collector, the ability to go around to all these different shops that might be directed toward what they're collecting," says Reddington-Hughes, noting that participating stores hang a flag outside the door to designate it as part of the trail. This country town is also home to the **Glebe House Museum and Gertrude Jekyll Garden (www.glebehouse museum.org).** The Georgian

The Glebe House Museum and Gertrude Jekyll Garden are filled with history.

colonial, built in 1740, is known as the place where the first election for the Episcopal Church took place in the United States. The history of this striking blue home doesn't stop there. In 1926 famed English horticultural designer and writer Gertrude Jekyll was hired to create a garden at the home, which has recently become a museum. "She was the most famous twentieth-century British gardner in England," says Connecticut tourism expert Janet Serra. It's not known why, but the plan was never fully executed. But after the plans were rediscovered in the late 1970s, the garden became a reality. The garden is open year-round; the house is fully open spring through the fall. Accessibility is limited; call the museum to discuss possible accommodation. The museum hosts several special events throughout the year, including an Earth Day Festival and All Hollow's Eve. Celebrities such as Dustin Hoffman, Stephen Sondheim, and Denis Leary have called this charming town home. Serra suggests a stop at **Woodbury Pewter** (**www.woodbury pewter.com**), a unique shop with more than five hundred handcrafted pewter pieces, from trays to barware.

Warren: Along with Kent and Washington, Warren is a town that borders beautiful **Lake Waramaug** (**portal.ct.gov/DEEP/State-Parks/Parks/ Lake-Waramaug-State-Park**), particularly stunning in the fall, when the foliage is reflected on the water's surface. Also don't miss a stop at **Hopkins Vineyard** (**www.hopkinsvineyard.com**). "We're one of the

All are welcome at Hopkins Vineyard, which produces a unique ice wine. Patricia Rowan

oldest wineries in Connecticut," says Hilary Criollo, part of the founding family and now president of the vineyard. Her parents started this endeavor in 1979. "We have a family-friendly vibe; we allow pets. We have a lovely picnic area. It's tented, with lots of tables and chairs. We have live music on Saturdays and Sundays throughout the season," she says. Since the pandemic, visitors have enjoyed sampling a wine flight more than participating in traditional wine tastings. "Customers can choose what wines they want on their flight. Then they take it, sit down, and relax," says Criollo, noting that customers receive samples of four wines. This farm winery is best known for its Cabernet Franc and Chardonnay, but it also produces a unique ice wine with origins in Germany. Ice wine is made after grapes freeze on the vine, appropriate for Connecticut's climate. "They are picked and pressed and made into a very sweet, rich dessert wine," says Criollo. Official tours stopped during the COVID pandemic, but Criollo is happy to give customers a spontaneous behind-the-scenes look at the vineyard. "You could say, 'All are welcome here,'" she says. In that spirit, this location is ADA compliant.

Glastonbury: This beautiful town along the Connecticut River offers a nice blend of farms and greenspace, along with upscale shops and restaurants. Every October, Glastonbury hosts a popular **Apple Harvest & Music Festival** (**www.glastonburyapplefest.com**) with concerts, food trucks, amusement rides, and a 5K road race that brings thousands of people of all ages out to Riverfront Park. Head to **Scott's Orchard & Nursery** (**www.scottsorchardandnursery.com**), a great spot for apple picking. In the fall, also find wagon rides, hay mazes, and plenty of pumpkins to peruse. Speaking of this favorite orange autumnal decoration, **Cavanna's Farm** (**www.facebook.com/ cavannasfarm1903**) in South Glastonbury is becoming a premier destination for kids and adults, thanks to its enthusiastic owner and his popular attraction. "I started the train in 2016 for agritourism to bring people into the farm," says

Glastonbury offers some great spots for picking apples and pumpkins.

Take a kayak excursion out of Riverfront Park.

John Cavanna, referring to his Gray Granite Railroad. "It's a diesel electric locomotive pulling two passenger cars." In the fall months, the train takes folks on a ten-minute ride to the pumpkin patch for a pickin' excursion. Later, there's also a haunted attraction, the Train of Torment, for kids twelve and over. The farm offers pick-your-own strawberries, raspberries, blackberries, and Christmas trees when the season is right. **Dondero Orchards (www.donderoorchards.com)**, also in South Glastonbury, is another favorite spot offering pick-your-own peaches, pears, apples, and plums in the fall. Find a similar scene at lovely **Belltown Hill Orchards (www.belltownhillorchards.com)**, with a vibrant season from mid-June through late October. For an adventure that's out of this world, head to the **Glastonbury Planetarium (www.glastonburyplanetarium.org)**, on the grounds of the Glastonbury–East Hartford Elementary Magnet School. On Thursday nights, the community is invited to learn about constellations, stars, and planets during shows for the public in the seventy-seat, forty-foot domed planetarium. And don't miss a hike out to **Blackledge Falls**, a waterfall on the Hebron–East Glastonbury line, part of an eighty-acre parcel of land that also offers fishing and pretty views. Lastly, **L.L.Bean (www.llbeanoutdoors.com/glastonbury-connecticut)** offers kayaking tours out of Riverfront Park in Glastonbury. Go out at sunrise or sunset. Folks can even enjoy a fall foliage tour.

Norwich: There's a lot to write about in this historic city, called the "Rose of New England." It's also notoriously known as Benedict Arnold's birthplace. Norwich is part of the **Last Green Valley Heritage Corridor** (see "Killingly" in the "Spring" section for more information). Tourism is part of the organization's mission statement. Every year, Walktober is a special time. "It starts with the autumnal equinox around the middle of September and goes through to the beginning of November. It consists of hundreds of walks, paddles, mountain biking meet-ups, and historic events," says Francesca Kefalas, assistant director of the heritage corridor. "People from all over the world come here." She says it's full of Native American, Revolutionary War, and industrial history. "The world's largest textile mills were here in Norwich and Willimantic. It's amazing what came out of this region," says Kefalas. The sixteen-acre **Mohegan Royal Burial Ground (www.mohegan.nsn.us/about/our-tribal-history/ historical-sites/mohegan-royal-burial-ground)** is a resting place for leaders of the Mohegan tribe and their families. The site also pays homage to Chief Uncas, who gave the original land for the settlement of the city. Also important to both the city and the Mohegan tribe is Uncas Leap, also known as Indian Leap or **Yantic Falls (walknorwich.org/ uncas-leap-trail/)**. The two-mile trail through this area, historically significant as the site of the Battle of Great Plains between the Mohegan and Narragansett tribes, features the ruins of a nineteenth-century mill, a gorge, and a beautiful waterfall. Other examples of history in this interesting city include the **Leffingwell House Museum (www .leffingwellhousemuseum.org)**, which dates back to 1675, a beautiful example of early American architecture. Folks can see this former tavern and home by booking a tour (appointment only) from April through October. The nearby **Joseph Carpenter Silversmith Shop**, also available for viewing, allows visitors to see an original forge. **Norwich Free Academy (www.nfaschool.org)**, one of the few endowed academies in New England, is an important spot in the city. Established in 1854, the academy aims to serve all students with a top-notch education. It's also home to the **Slater Memorial Museum (www.slatermuseum.org)**, which has been around for more than 135 years. "It's really uniquely positioned in the country, because we're one of only two museums to be located on the campus of a high school in the United States," says Museum Director Dayne Rugh, noting that the museum originally featured a collection of plaster casts that were duplicates of famous works. Today it contains original work from all around the globe,

See a mix of global and local art at the Slater Memorial Museum. Slater Memorial Museum/Tim Cook

including Africa, Asia, and South America. "We also have a very large collection of local art made right here in Norwich, made in Connecticut," says Rugh. This includes maritime art that pays homage to members of the Mohegan tribe who contributed to shipbuilding in the area. Each year, the museum hosts an annual Autumn Artisan Craft Show with handcrafted, locally made goods. The museum is accessible for those with mobility issues.

Monroe: See the bright colors of fall reflected off the water at Great Hollow Lake, part of **William E. Wolf Park (www.monroect.myrec .com)** in this family-oriented town, filled with lovely shops, restaurants, and outdoor recreation. Head to the **Webb Mountain Discovery Zone (www.webbmountaindiscoveryzone.wildapricot.org)**, with 171 acres of land. This destination was born in 2007 as a result of the Leave No Child Inside movement that swept the nation. "We're a nature center that focuses on children's outdoor education. We have over four miles of trails that families can use, free of charge," says Director Tom Ellbogen. "We also have scavenger hunts, free of charge, created by top experts in the state of Connecticut." Folks can pick up a scavenger hunt card and trail map at the park. The hunt links to the park's interpretive trail system. Participants look for nature items such as moss, lichen, quartz, and a quarry. They even search for a kiln and an old farm road. "It's trying to engage children to observe what's around them. That's really what we're focused on, making the outdoors exciting, fun, and interesting,"

Explore the trails while riding a horse at Blue Spruce Farm.

says Ellbogen, who notes that although the early parts of the trails are accessible, folks will eventually encounter roots and rocks along the way. Also enjoy nature with a gentle behemoth by your side. Embark on a scenic wooded trail ride at **Blue Spruce Farm** (**www.bluespruce horseriding.com**). "We take people in the forest for a forty-five-minute ride. It's a slow walk. We have a large pond. If they feel like going in the water, they can. It's very refreshing. There's also a picnic area for the public if they do a service with us," says owner Rosanne Plavnicky, who has been in business for fifty years. "We also have antique tractor rides through the forest. It's almost like another world. There are trees all around you. It's a nice feeling being out here." This wooded spot, with thirteen rescued horses, also offers therapeutic riding opportunities for those of all abilities, along with hayrides and riding lessons.

Roxbury: Take a day trip out to this charming town, nestled in the Litchfield Hills in the northwest corner of Connecticut. The air here feels particularly fresh as visitors take in expansive views from green fields lined with stone walls and old wooden fences. It was the longtime home of Pulitzer Prize– and Tony award–winning playwright Arthur Miller, author of *The Crucible* and *Death of a Salesman*. To pay your respects to this influential and prolific writer, visit his gravesite at **Roxbury Central Cemetery**, where folks have placed books of his work and stones. Also

Left: Leave a remembrance at Pulitzer Prize–winning author Arthur Miller's gravesite. Right: See the remnants of a blast furnace from the iron ore industry at Mine Hill Preserve. Janet Serra

check out a unique spot called **Mine Hill Preserve (www.roxbury landtrust.org/preserves/mine-hill/)**, the site of an iron mine and furnace complex from the 1860s. This National Historic Landmark is run by the **Roxbury Land Trust (www.roxburylandtrust.org)**. "It's the remnants of a blast furnace from the iron ore industry," says Connecticut tourism expert Janet Serra, who created a walking tour of this destination. "On a hot summer day, you can feel the cold air coming up from the mines." She says visitors can't go into the mines themselves but can see the remaining pieces via a trail that extends 3.5 miles in this 360-acre preserve. Learn the facts about the area's industrial history through interpretive signage. The **Shepaug River** runs through this scenic town, providing lovely views along main roads. There are even spots to stop to take in the beauty.

Smell fresh air and see bucolic scenes in the beautiful town of Roxbury.

North Haven: Connecticut has a vibrant summer and fall fair scene. And this wholesome town with agricultural roots is home to the **North Haven Fair (www.northhaven-fair.com)**, a longtime staple of fun. "It dates back to World War II and has been a draw the weekend after Labor Day for many decades in the same location, right off exit 12 from Interstate 91," says Ray Andrewsen of the **Quinnipiac Chamber of Commerce (www.quinncham.com)**. Find great fair food like cotton candy and corn dogs, along with animals, concerts, and rides. Andrewsen, who grew up in town, says the area sports an all-American feel. "North Haven is that classic, 'Kid goes out in the street and plays wiffle ball' type of town," he says. Downtown is filled with great shops and restaurants, along with a historic site—an eighteenth- and nineteenth-century burial ground, surrounded by old homes and a long-standing church. Find great opportunities to enjoy nature at **Quinnipiac River State Park (portal .ct.gov/DEEP/State-Parks/Parks/Quinnipiac-River-State-Park)**, great for hiking, and **Wharton Brook State Park (portal.ct.gov/DEEP/State -Parks/Parks/Wharton-Brook-State-Park)**, a popular spot for picnicking and fishing.

See impressive animals, like this llama, at the North Haven Fair. Mike Kennedy, North Haven Fair Association

Hamden: Appreciate all the colors of this gorgeous season at **Sleeping Giant State Park (portal.ct.gov/DEEP/State-Parks/Parks/Sleeping -Giant-State-Park)**, named for a landscape that actually looks like a large man lying down. Upon entering the park, straight across the street from **Quinnipiac University (www.qu.edu)**, see an open field with new grass and baby trees, where folks now kick a soccer ball or throw a Frisbee. This area has been cleaned up and revamped after it was decimated by a tornado in 2018. Walk a little farther and find the Tower Trail, a really doable jaunt to the top of Mount Carmel. Round-trip, it's 3.1 miles long, which takes about an hour and a half. While the ascent causes a sweat, it's not that hard, and it's largely shaded, with views of ledges and interesting glacial features. Once at the top, find a stone observation tower. Walk through its narrow halls along ramps and up a few levels to find panoramic views, including the city of New Haven and Long Island Sound. But that's not the only way to hike Sleeping Giant. "There's an additional thirty-two miles of backcountry trails, which is more of your traditional hiking trails that crisscross the Giant in almost a grid formation, so it's easy to navigate and get to all the more hidden

The most popular path to the top of Sleeping Giant State Park is easy to navigate.

The stone observation tower atop Sleeping Giant State Park has narrow halls and ramps.

parts of the giant," says Aaron Lefland of the **Sleeping Giant Park Association** (**www.sgpa.org**), which in the 1920s purchased the land to save it from quarrying and then transferred the land to the state. A more difficult trail leads visitors to a lovely gorge cascade and waterfall. The park has accessible parking and picnic areas. Note: Cars with Connecticut license plates can enter state parks without drivers having to pay a fee. "Every time you renew your vehicle, you have a fifteen-dollar Passport to the Parks fee, which gives you access through your license plate to any park in our state for free," says Ryan Snide, president of the **Friends of Connecticut State Parks** (**www.friendsctstateparks.org**). There are also great hiking opportunities at **West Rock Ridge State Park** (**portal.ct .gov/DEEP/State-Parks/Parks/West-Rock-Ridge-State-Park**) on the New

Haven–Hamden line. For more outdoor recreation, head to the **Brooksvale Park and Nature Trail** (**www.brooksvale.org**), a park and sanctuary where folks can hike the trails and see barnyard animals. Also check out the **Eli Whitney Museum and Workshop** (**www .eliwhitney.org**), called "an experimental learning workshop"

The top of Sleeping Giant State Park affords views to Long Island Sound.

for kids and adults. Research shows that children thrive when they have time to be curious and explore, which is what they're encouraged to do during walk-in hours and special programs. In fact, the museum offers a list of "1,000 Experiments to Try Before You Grow Up." Eli Whitney, inventor of the cotton gin, has become a controversial figure in New Haven in recent years. There have even been suggestions of renaming Whitney Avenue because of his involvement in this industry that expanded slavery. The museum is wheelchair accessible.

Cheshire: Who knew? While researching this lovely town, I discovered that it's known as the "Bedding Plant Capital of Connecticut." At first I thought this meant sheets and comforters! But no, the name comes from the large number of farms in the area growing and selling annuals and perennials in "beds." For outdoor recreation, take the family to the beautiful **Farmington Canal State Park Trail (portal.ct.gov/DEEP/ State-Parks/Parks/Farmington-Canal-State-Park-Trail/Overview)**, which stretches 5.5 miles and passes through Cheshire and other towns. This trail offers great views along the canal, which was a pathway for commerce from 1828 to 1847. The area includes **Lock 12 Historical Park (www.cheshirect.org/government/departments_and_divisions/ recreation/lock_12_historic_park)**, where folks can see a restored 150-year-old canal lock, which was basically an elevator for lowering and raising boats in and out of the water. And that's not all. Head to **Roaring Brook Park (www.cheshirelandtrust.org/copy-of-fresh-meadows)**, owned by the Town of Cheshire and the State of Connecticut, for great hiking and a chance to see a gorgeous waterfall. Cheshire is home to another unique gem of a destination, the **Barker Character, Comic & Cartoon Museum (www.barkermuseum.com)**. "It has over eighty thousand toys and collectibles from 1873 to present day," says General Manager Karen St. Clair. "We have everything from tin toys to items about Popeye. We have so many different toys, ones you had as a kid or wished you had as a kid." Herb and Gloria Barker founded this museum in 1997 as an homage to those everyday items that bring us a sense of nostalgia. Remember those *Scooby-Doo* and *Charlie's Angels* lunch box–thermos sets? You might just find them here in this personal collection of treasures. The first floor, bursting with items, is accessible to all, but getting up to the second floor will present a challenge for those with mobility issues. "It's a great place because it starts conversations," says St. Clair, noting that families have a ball as kids discover and parents

Get a dose of nostalgia at the Barker Character, Comic & Cartoon Museum. Barker Character, Comic and Cartoon Museum

rediscover. "We're all affected by toys." Think about the movie *Toy Story*. There's also an animation art gallery and gift shop next door. "It has animation artwork from Disney and Warner Brothers. We also sell Funko Pops," says St. Clair of the popular figurines depicting a plethora of characters from the *Harry Potter* franchise to *Star Wars* heroes. At this museum in 2001, I had the pleasure of meeting and interviewing Myron Waldman, the man who animated the legendary character Betty Boop. He was a delight, sketching a picture of Betty that still hangs on a wall in my home today.

Trumbull: This charming town offers an abundance of fun for families, beginning with outdoor recreation. The **Trumbull Nature and Arts Center** (**www.trumbullnatureandartscenter.org**) is a great spot for learning facts while getting the body moving. "We like to call ourselves a source for environmental education. We provide programs for students and families," says director Sheryl Baumann. Folks can stop by, use the playground and hiking trails, or embark on some pond exploration. The center also provides a bevy of programs like "Intro to Archery," "Wreath Making," or "Build a Bat

Discover the Science and Adventure Trail at the Trumbull Nature and Arts Center. Sheryl Baumann

House." Visitors can also preregister online for a unique opportunity to use the new Science and Adventure Trail. "Families will visit TNAC and spend time outside, conducting hands-on environmental science experiments and activities. Each family will receive a trail map and guide book, filled with instructions and photos," says Baumann. "It's to get families outside, doing something fun and working together. It's like an enhanced walk through the woods with stops along the way." Participants will learn about things like solar- and hydropower. They may be asked to build a bird's nest. At the end, they get their guidebook stamped and certified. TNAC features mostly flat trails. Some areas are accessible for wheelchairs and strollers. There is an accessible ramp for restrooms inside the building. Also check out **SeaQuest** (**www.visitseaquest.com/ connecticut/**) at the Westfield Trumbull Mall, a twenty-thousand-square-foot wheelchair-accessible aquarium that's home to more than one thousand animals from five continents. Kids can explore touch tanks and interactive exhibits. Have you ever donned a virtual reality headset and disappeared into another world? Well, you can at **Xperiment Virtual Reality** (**www.xperimentvr.com**), a state-of-the-art location offering all sorts of interactive experiences for those of all ages. The ADA-compliant location also features virtual escape rooms and racing simulators.

UNIQUE OUTINGS FOR FALL

The **Connecticut Wine Trail** (**www.ctwine.com**), stretching from the Litchfield Hills to Long Island Sound, was established in 1988 as a way to promote agritourism and celebrate the state's growing industry. And fall is the best time of year to "taste the adventure" and sample the varieties while enjoying the unique vibes at the fifty vineyards in our state that really work in collaboration rather than competition.

Make a stop at Gouveia Vineyards during an excursion along the Connecticut Wine Trail.

Autumn means harvest season, when the green and purple fruit adorn the vines, ready to begin the long process of becoming Chardonnay or Cabernet Franc. Many of the vineyards provide tours and sampling, along with information about bottling and labeling. An online passport program, sponsored by the Connecticut Farm Wineries and the Connecticut Department of Agriculture, makes it fun and easy to traverse the trail. Participants can download an app on their phone, visit wineries, gather stamps, and enter to win prizes. We've talked about many of the participating vineyards in this book, but also be sure to check out ones not described, such as **Hawk Ridge Winery** (**www.hawkridgewinery.net**) in Watertown, the **Jones Winery** (**www.jonesfamilyfarms.com**) in Shelton, and **Sunset Meadow Vineyards** (**www.sunsetmeadowvineyards.com**) in Goshen. One of the most well-known vineyards, the **Jonathan Edwards Winery** (**www.jedwardswinery.com**) hosts a popular Harvest Festival each year in October with bands, food trucks, artisan tents, and more. Also every fall, the staff at **Gouveia Vineyards** (**www .gouveiavineyards.com**) invites four hundred volunteers on-site to help pick grapes from the thirty acres of vines. The Gouveia family brings out the crush pad and press so that folks can see exactly how the wine-making process takes place.

From one locally made drink to another! Nothing beats a trip to an old-fashioned cider mill during the colorful autumn months in Connecticut. And our state boasts some lovely spots. Head to the **Old Cider Mill** (**www.riverviewfarmsct.com**) in Glastonbury, considered the oldest continuously operating cider mill in the United States, boasting a petting zoo and an apple fritter stand (yum!). **Hogan's Cider Mill** (**www.hoganscidermill.com**) in Burlington has been producing the sweet drink in its historic barn since the early 1900s. Hard cider, served in a family-friendly taproom, has also been added to the menu. Stop at

Hogan's Cider Mill in Burlington has been producing the sweet drink in its historic barn since the early 1900s. Hogan's Cider Mill

Park Lane Cider Mill during an autumn tour of the New Milford area, full of New England charm. I have produced many news stories at **B. F. Clyde's Cider Mill** (**www.clydescidermill .com**) in Mystic, the oldest steam-powered mill in the United States. Every year, folks gaze upon the process as apples are mashed, strained, pressed, and made into juice. Also be sure to check out **Beardsley's Cider Mill and Orchards** (**www.beardsleyscidermill.com**) in Shelton, also a great place to pick apples and buy Thanksgiving pies.

Connecticut is full of one-of-a-kind locations and events, and guess what? Find one in Scotland in October. The **Highland Festival & Games** (**www .scotlandgames.org**) at Waldo Farm features music, food, and authentic Highlands dress. "They have the largest and oldest Scottish Festival in the state of Connecticut. It's been going on for thirty-eight years," says Jill St. Clair of the Eastern Regional Tourism District. "It's the most amazing thing; it features competitions. People come from all around the United States to compete in the old Scottish games." Pets are not allowed at this festival. Buy tickets online in advance.

The Highland Festival & Games at Waldo Farm features music, food, and authentic Highlands dress. Reggie Patchell

You've seen it before. That label on cartons of milk and other dairy products in grocery store refrigerators featuring a serious bovine standing in front of a stone wall. Well, that symbolizes the **Farmer's Cow** (**www.thefarmerscow.com**), based right here in Connecticut. "The Farmer's Cow is a group of farms that is active in trying to promote agriculture in Connecticut, letting people know agriculture is still alive in the state. It was really based on preserving farmland," says Jim Smith, on the board of the Farmer's Cow and a co-owner of **Cushman Farms** in Franklin. This consortium of six family dairy farms now sells milk, ice cream, and eggs throughout southern New England and New York. Visitors are invited to witness the process by taking tours at spots like **Graywall Farms** in Lebanon, where a wagon ride first takes visitors out into the fields. They then see into the barn, where the hardworking Holstein cows live in comfort. A tour includes a look at the milking parlor, where six hundred cows are milked for an incredible four hours! The final stop is the tank room. About twenty-eight thousand pounds of milk is produced in this high-tech dairy each and every day. The tours were paused during the pandemic but

The Farmer's Cow is a group of six farms, including Graywall Farms in Lebanon.

resumed in the fall of 2023. "We always have great turnouts for the farm tours," says Smith, so glad they are back. Smith says this co-op of farms educates while also creating jobs for folks in the state. Each year, the Farmer's Cow produces limited-edition flavored milk that's become quite popular. Think blueberry— and even root beer! Other farms include **Fairvue Farms** (*www.fairvuefarms.com*) in Woodstock; **Hytone Farm** in Coventry; and Hebron's **Mapleleaf Farm** and **Fort Hill Farms** (*www.forthillfarms.com*) in Thompson, which features a popular corn maze every fall.

Take tours of the Farmer's Cow operation, showing visitors the inner workings of a dairy farm. The Farmer's Cow

It's a sport you don't hear too much about, but there are some great options for viewing polo right here in Connecticut, from summer into fall. Sure, watching this sport means appreciating the partnership of the player and the horse. But it's also about enjoying a sophisticated afternoon at the grounds. Yes, harken back to the famous stomping of the divots scene in Pretty Woman (am I dating myself?) and you'll conjure up images full of style, fashion, and fun. In recent years the **Greenwich Polo Club** (*www.greenwich polocclub.com*) at Conyers Farm has made an effort to make viewing this competitive sport more accessible and affordable for everyone. It's one of the few sports where women and men can play together. Kids of all ages are welcome, as well as dogs on leashes. Other options for great viewing of this sport include the **Farmington Polo Club** (*www.farmingtonpoloclub.com*) and **Giant Valley Polo Club** (*www .giantvalleypolo.com*) in Hamden.

Find style, fashion, fun, and impressive athleticism during a match at Greenwich Polo Club. Greenwich Polo

It's always the right season to visit the **PEZ Visitor Center** (**us.pez.com**) in Orange! This colorful candy emporium claims to hold the largest, most complete collection of PEZ memorabilia in the entire world. Walk into the center to see antique and modern dispensers bearing the likenesses of everyone from Wonder Woman to the Disney princesses and Darth Vader. Also see sports-themed dispensers. Take a self-guided tour through this four-thousand-square-foot space to see into the production floor. Also get a good look at the world's largest PEZ

The PEZ Visitor Center shows a unique view of Americana.

dispenser. It's a unique, vibrant place, full of families having fun. Folks can also learn about this company, which was founded in Austria. The company's first manufacturing plant was built in Orange in 1973. The building is accessible, with wide passageways and an elevator.

I hope you've enjoyed learning about our state's various trails, meant to boost enjoyment and awareness of our resources along with tourism. So let's finish with a look at **Connecticut's Art Trail** (**www.ctarttrail.org**), run by a nonprofit group that is a compilation of twenty-three area museums and historic locations. Purchase a passport that then provides free admission to all of these sites. The trail includes destinations profiled in this book, such as the **New Britain Museum of American Art** and **Weir Farm National Historical Park**.

Places like Weir Farm and the Yale Center for British Art are on Connecticut's Art Trail.

But it also includes others, such as the **Bush-Holley House Museum** in Greenwich, the site of Connecticut's first Impressionist art colony. Learn all about the **Silvermine Arts Center** in New Canaan, one of the oldest art communities in the country. Also check out the **Eastern Art Gallery** in Willimantic on the campus of Eastern Connecticut State University, featuring a collection of contemporary art. Have fun exploring!

Acknowledgments

Thank you to all the wonderful state parks and museums mentioned in this book, along with CT Visit, the Connecticut Tourism Office, for providing the public with such comprehensive information on websites, which I referred to during my writing process. I want to profusely thank each and every person who returned my call or email and set time aside for an interview about these rich and varied places. Their information, passion, and perspective make *Around Every Corner of Connecticut* so much more than a guidebook. They give the passages life and personality. I couldn't be more grateful for their participation, enthusiasm, and support. Also, I'd like to acknowledge my two places of employment, Fox 61 and News 8, for encouraging my tourism reporting over my career. It was fun to return to some of my previous assignments to cover them in a new way for this book. Thank you to my husband, Paul, and two sons, Sam and Ben. And I can't forget the fur babies, Lucy and Jack! For years, this fun crew has gotten me out and about, exploring new destinations. Lastly, thank you to the readers who accompanied me on this adventure. I really enjoyed traipsing all over, revisiting favorite spots and discovering new ones. I hope I've inspired you to find a museum you've never toured or a state park you've never explored. Trust me, the journey isn't over! 'Til next time . . .

Index